Complete Air F

250 Simple a

Air Fryer Recipes

for Oil-Free Everyday Meals

Sara Parker

Contents

Introduction

I cook because I love to cook. This is my passion and I cannot live without cooking. All this goes from childhood when I lived with my parents. I remember my mother always cooked various delicious dishes using many devices. Air Fryer was one of these kitchen appliances that helped my mom create superb meals for the whole family.

A lot of time has passed since that moment. Now I'm living separately for a long time, but my love for cooking only grew from year to year. Air Fryer became one of my favorite kitchen appliances. The key advantage of this device is that I can cook healthy, oil-free and delicious dishes without spending time on it. I just need to choose one of my favorite recipes, prepare & combine ingredients and transfer all of these to the Air Fryer! That's all! Amazing, delicious, and healthy oil-free meals ready for me and my family!

In this cookbook you will find a great variety of recipes for all occasions. You will find recipes for healthy breakfasts, easy snacks and sides, separate potato and vegetable-based recipes, poultry, meat and seafood meals, and of course, yummy desserts! All that you lacked in your other cookbooks you can find in HERE!

Benefits of the Air Fryer

Air Fryer is one of my favorite appliances and it has numerous benefits. All of you know that with the help of the Air Fryer you can easily prepare oil-free meals. But there are also many other benefits and while cooking you'll find more and more advantages of using this amazing device!

Oil-free Cooking
You do not need to use more than couple tablespoons of fat or vegetable oil while cooking dishes in the air fryer. In result, you get healthier roasted food which not soaking in unhealthy fat.

Easy Cooking
It not needed to watch over your pan while frying your dinner. You just put ingredients into the fryer basket, set cooking preferences, push couple buttons and wait for the meals to get prepared.

Fast Preparation
It is faster to cook in the air fryer that anywhere else. This is due to high temperature air circulating inside the fryer basket. Hot air passes through the meals making it ready faster.

Cleaning Fast
Most of the air fryer details and cooking chamber are dishwasher safe. You can easily clean them either with a soapy sponge or in the dishwasher.

Various Meals
You can not only roast with the help of air fryer. You can easily bake, grill, stew in it too!

Cooking Measurement Conversion Chart

Liquid Measures

1 gal = 4 qt = 8 pt = 16 cups = 128 fl oz
½ gal = 2 qt = 4 pt = 8 cups = 64 fl oz
¼ gal = 1 qt = 2 pt = 4 cups = 32 fl oz
½ qt = 1 pt = 2 cups = 16 fl oz
¼ qt = ½ pt = 1 cup = 8 fl oz

Dry Measures

1 cup = 16 Tbsp = 48 tsp = 250ml
¾ cup = 12 Tbsp = 36 tsp = 175ml
⅔ cup = 10 ⅔ Tbsp = 32 tsp = 150ml
½ cup = 8 Tbsp = 24 tsp = 125ml
⅓ cup = 5 ⅓ Tbsp = 16 tsp = 75ml
¼ cup = 4 Tbsp = 12 tsp = 50ml
⅛ cup = 2 Tbsp = 6 tsp = 30ml
1 Tbsp = 3 tsp = 15ml

Dash or Pinch or Speck = less than ⅛ tsp

Quickies

1 fl oz = 30 ml
1 oz = 28.35 g
1 lb = 16 oz (454 g)
1 kg = 2.2 lb
1 quart = 2 pints

U.S. / Canadian

U.S.	Canadian
¼ tsp	1.25 mL
½ tsp	2.5 mL
1 tsp	5 mL
1 Tbl	15 mL
¼ cup	50 mL
⅓ cup	75 mL
½ cup	125 mL
⅔ cup	150 mL
¾ cup	175 mL
1 cup	250 mL
1 quart	1 liter

Recipe Abbreviations

Cup = c or C
Fluid = fl
Gallon = gal
Ounce = oz
Package = pkg
Pint = pt
Pound = lb or #
Quart = qt
Square = sq
Tablespoon = T or Tbl
   or TBSP or TBS
Teaspoon = t or tsp

Fahrenheit (°F) to Celcius (°C)

$°C = (°F - 32) \times 5/9$

Fahrenheit (°F)	Celcius (°C)
32 °F	0 °C
40 °F	4 °C
140 °F	60 °C
150 °F	65 °C
160 °F	70 °C
225 °F	107 °C
250 °F	121 °C
275 °F	135 °C
300 °F	150 °C
325 °F	165 °C
350 °F	177 °C
375 °F	190 °C
400 °F	205 °C
425 °F	220 °C
450 °F	230 °C
475 °F	245 °C
500 °F	260 °C

OVEN TEMPERATURES

WARMING: 200 °F
VERY SLOW: 250 °F - 275 °F
SLOW: 300 °F - 325 °F
MODERATE: 350 °F - 375 °F
HOT: 400 °F - 425 °F
VERY HOT: 450 °F - 475 °F

*Some measurements were rounded

Optimize your Metabolism

Optimizing metabolism is a main key to weight loss. It means that you will burn more calories even when you're rest, even without physical workout. Here's useful chart with 12 main foods which will boost your metabolism. Just include as many of these products as you can in your daily diet and get a great opportunity to control your weight and create a perfect body!

Weight Loss Diet Tips that Really Work

Please also check main weight loss tips which can help you control body weight.

KEEP YOURSELF HYDRATED

NEVER MISS BREAKFAST

EAT MORE FRUITS

GET ON THE SCALE

TIPS THAT WORK

WATCH YOUR ALCOHOL INTAKE

TURN OFF THE TV

GET ENOUGH SLEEP

SUGAR FREE

BEWARE OF "DIET" & "SUGAR-FREE" FOODS

Breakfast Recipes

Delicious Air Fryer Potato Gratin

Prep time: 15 minutes, cook time: 20 minutes, serves: 3

Ingredients

- 1 pound potato, pilled
- 2 oz milk
- 2 oz cream
- Ground pepper
- Nutmeg to taste
- 2 oz cheese, grated

Directions

1. Slice potatoes.
2. Take the large bowl and combine milk and cream. Season to taste with salt, ground pepper, and nutmeg.
3. Cover the potato slices with milk mixture.
4. Preheat the Air Fryer to 370°F.
5. Transfer covered potato slices to the quiche pan. Pour the rest of the milk mixture on the top of the potatoes.
6. Evenly cover the potatoes with grated cheese.
7. Place the quiche pan into the Air Fryer and cook for 15-20 minutes until nicely golden.

Breakfast Sandwich

Prep time: 5 minutes, cook time: 7 minutes, serves: 1

Ingredients

- 1 egg, beaten
- 2 streaky bacon stripes
- 1 English muffin
- A pinch of salt and pepper

Directions

1. Beat 1 egg into an oven proof cup or bowl.
2. Preheat the Air fryer to 390°F
3. Place the egg in the cup, bacon stripes and muffin to the fryer and cook for 6-7 minutes.
4. Get the sandwich together and enjoy.

Delicious English Breakfast

Prep time: 5 minutes, cook time: 13-15 minutes, serves: 4

Ingredients

- 8 chestnut mushrooms
- 8 tomatoes
- 4 eggs
- 1 clove garlic, halved
- 4 slices smoked bacon, crushed
- 4 chipolatas
- 7 oz baby leaf spinach
- 1 tablespoon extra virgin olive oil
- Salt and ground black pepper to taste

Directions

1. Preheat the Air fryer to 390 F
2. Place the mushrooms, tomatoes, and garlic in a round tin. Season with salt and ground pepper and spray with olive oil. Place the tin, bacon, and chipolatas in the cooking basket of your Air Fryer. Cook for 10 minutes.
3. Meanwhile, wilt the spinach in a microwave or by pouring boiling water through it in a sieve. Drain well.
4. Add the spinach to the tin and crack in the eggs. Reduce the temperature to 300 F and cook for couple minutes more, until the eggs are prepared.
5. Sprinkle with freshly chopped herbs you prefer and serve.

Easy Cooking Toasted Cheese

Prep time: 10 minutes, cook time: 6 minutes, serves 2

Ingredients

- 2 sliced white bread
- 4 oz cheese, grated
- Little piece of butter

Directions

1. At first, toast the bread in the toaster
2. Once toasted spread the butter on bread pieces
3. Cover with grated cheese
4. Preheat the Air Fryer to 350°F
5. Place covered bread slices into the Fryer and cook for 4-6 minutes
6. Serve with your favorite sauce or without it.

Morning Vegetables on Toast

Prep time: 7 minutes, cook time: 11 minutes, serves 4

Ingredients

- 4 slices French or Italian bread
- 1 red bell pepper, cut into strips
- 1 cup sliced button or cremini mushrooms
- 1 small yellow squash, sliced
- 2 green onions, sliced
- 1 tablespoon olive oil
- 2 tablespoons softened butter;
- ½ cup soft goat cheese

Directions

1. Sprinkle the air fryer with olive oil and preheat the appliance to 350 F. Add red pepper, mushrooms, squash, and green onions, mix well and cook for 7 minutes or until the vegetables are tender, shaking the basket once during cooking time.
2. Transfer vegetables to a plate and set aside.
3. Spread bread slices with butter and place in the air fryer, butter-side up. Toast for 2 to 4 minutes or until golden brown.
4. Spread the goat cheese on the toasted bread and top with the vegetables.
5. Serve warm.

Spinach and Cheese Omelette

Prep time: 5 minutes, cook time: 8 minutes, serves: 2

Ingredients

- 4 large eggs
- ½ cup Cheddar cheese, shredded
- 3 tablespoons fresh spinach, chopped
- Salt to taste

Directions

1. In the large bowl whisk the eggs. Place the eggs in a flat oven safe form. Stir in shredded cheese and spinach, and season with salt.
2. Preheat the air fryer to 380 F and cook for about 7-8 minutes, until ready.

Bacon and Avocado Mix Recipe

Prep time: 5 minutes, cook time: 10 minutes, serves: 3

Ingredients

- Buns - 1 small pack
- ½ small squash, shredded
- 1 medium bell pepper, chopped
- 2 bacon slices
- 1 small avocado, chopped
- 1 tablespoon humus
- 1 cup Cheddar cheese, shredded

Directions

1. Add shredded squash, bell pepper and bacon in a bowl. Stir in avocado and humus. Stir well all the ingredients, then add cheese.
2. Make small round patties and turn on the air fryer to 300 F.
3. Place the patties in the air fryer and cook for 10 minutes.
4. When done, place the patty in a bun and enjoy!

Breakfast Air Fryer Jacket Potatoes Loaded with Cheesy Topping

Prep time: 6 minutes, cook time: 20 minutes, serves: 4

Ingredients

- 4 medium-sized Russell potatoes
- 1 tablespoon unsalted butter
- 4 tablespoon sour cream
- 1 tablespoon chives, chopped
- 2 oz cheese, grated
- Salt and freshly ground black pepper to taste

Directions

1. Prepare four medium-sized potatoes, wash them and dry with kitchen towels. Stab potatoes with a fork so that they can breathe.
2. Preheat the Air Fryer at 370 F. Place potatoes into the Fryer basket and cook for 15 minutes, until tender and golden.
3. Meanwhile, prepare your filling. In the medium mixing bowl combine sour cream with grated cheese and chives until it is equally mixed.
4. When the jacket potatoes are cooked open them up and spread with butter followed by your topping mixture.
5. Serve and enjoy!

Baked Eggs in Avocado Nests

Prep time: 5 minutes, cook time: 20 minutes, serves: 2

Ingredients

- 1 large avocado, halved
- 2 eggs
- 4 grape tomato, halved
- 2 teaspoon chives, chopped
- A pinch of sea salt and black pepper

Directions

1. Cut avocado in half length-wise. Remove the pit and widen the hole in each half by scraping out the avocado flesh with the help of the spoon.
2. Place avocado halves in a small oven proof baking dish cut side up.
3. Beat an egg into each half of avocado. Season with salt and pepper.
4. Cook for about 10-15 minutes in 370°F into the Air Fryer.
5. Top with grape tomato halves and chives. Enjoy!

French Toast Sticks

Prep time: 5 minutes, cook time: 5-8 minutes, serves: 2

Ingredients

- 4 pieces bread, sliced
- 2 tablespoon soft butter
- 2 eggs, beaten
- ¼ teaspoon cinnamon
- ¼ teaspoon nutmeg
- ¼ teaspoon ground cloves
- Icing sugar for garnish
- A pinch of salt

Directions

1. It the bowl beat two eggs, sprinkle with salt, cinnamon, nutmeg and ground cloves.
2. Butter both sides of bread and cut into stripes.
3. Preheat the Air Fryer to 350-370 F
4. Dip each bread strip into the egg mixture and then put into the air fryer.
5. Cook for about 5-8 minutes until eggs are cooked and bread become golden.
6. Garnish with icing sugar and top with cream or maple syrup (as for your desire).

Morning Cinnamon Toasts

Prep time: 5 minutes, cook time: 5 minutes, serves: 4-5

Ingredients

- 10 medium bread slices
- 1 pack salted butter
- 4 tablespoons sugar
- 2 teaspoons ground cinnamon
- ½ teaspoon vanilla extract

Directions

1. Place salted butter to a mixing bowl and add sugar, cinnamon, and vanilla extract. Mix well and spread the mixture over bread slices.
2. Preheat the air fryer to 380 F and place bread slices to a fryer.
3. Cook for 4-5 minutes and serve hot!

Air Fryer Spinach Frittata

Prep time: 5 minutes, cook time: 10-12 minutes, serves: 2

Ingredients

- 1 small onion, minced
- 1/3 pack (4oz) spinach
- 3 eggs, beaten
- 3 oz mozzarella cheese
- 1 tablespoon olive oil
- Salt and pepper to taste

Directions

1. Preheat the Air fryer to 370 F
2. In a baking pan heat the oil for about a minute.
3. Add minced onions into the pan and cook for 2-3 minutes.
4. Add spinach and cook for about 3-5 minutes to about half cooked. They may look a bit dry but it is ok, just keep frying with the oil.
5. In the large bowl whisk the beaten eggs, season with salt and pepper and sprinkle with cheese. Pour the mixture into a baking pan.
6. Place the pan in the air fryer and cook for 6-8 minutes or until cooked.

Breakfast Frittata

Prep time: 5 minutes, cook time: 10 minutes, serves: 2

Ingredients

- 4 large eggs
- ¼ cup skimmed milk
- ¼ pound Italian Sausage
- 4 cherry tomatoes cut in half
- 2 tablespoons chopped parsley
- Salt and black pepper, to taste
- 1 tablespoon olive oil

Directions

1. Place cut sausage and cherry tomatoes to a fryer basket and cook at 360 F for 3-5 minutes, stirring once while cooking.
2. Meanwhile, combine eggs, milk and parsley in a mixing bowl. Season the mixture with salt and pepper and whisk well.
3. Pour the egg mixture to an air fryer and cook for another 5 minutes, until ready.
4. Enjoy easy and healthy breakfast.

Classic English Tuna Sandwiches

Prep time 8 minutes, cook time: 10 minutes, serves: 4

Ingredients

- 1 can (6 oz) tuna
- 4 tablespoons mayonnaise
- 1-2 tablespoons mustard
- 1 tablespoon freshly squeezed lemon juice
- 1 small onion, sliced
- 4 English muffins
- 4 tablespoons unsalted butter,
- 8 slices Cheddar cheese

Directions

1. In a large mixing bowl combine drained canned tuna, mustard, mayo, lemon juice and minced onion. Season with black pepper and salt, to taste.
2. Cut English muffins on halves and butter one side.
3. Preheat the air fryer to 380 F and cook muffins for 3-4 minutes, until golden. Open the fryer and top each muffin with cheese. Return to the air fryer and cook for another 3-4 minutes, until the cheese melts.
4. Remove muffins from the fryer, top with tuna mixture and serve.

Fried Eggs with Ham

Prep time: 5 minutes, cook time: 10-15 minutes, serves: 2

Ingredients

- 4 eggs
- 2 oz (nearly 2 thin slices) ham
- 2 teaspoon butter
- 2 tablespoon heavy cream
- 3 tablespoon Parmesan cheese, grated
- 2 teaspoon fresh chives, chopped
- A pinch of smoked paprika
- Salt and ground black pepper to taste

Directions

1. Grease the pie pan with butter and line the bottom with ham slices. Make the bottom and sides of the pie pan completely covered with ham.
2. In a small bowl beat 1 egg, add heavy cream, a pinch of salt and 1/8 teaspoon ground pepper. Whisk to combine.
3. Pour this egg mixture over the ham and beat remaining 3 eggs over top.
4. Season with salt and ground pepper, sprinkle with Parmesan cheese.
5. Preheat the Air Fryer to 320-350°F
6. Place the pie pan into the cooking basket and cook for 12 minutes.
7. When finished, remove fried eggs from the pie pan with the help of spatula and transfer to the plate. Season with smoked paprika and chopped chives.

Easy Breakfast Casserole

Prep time: 15 minutes, cook time: 25-30 minutes, serves: 5-6

Ingredients

- 1 pound hot breakfast sausage
- ½ bag (15 oz) frozen hash browns, shredded
- 1 cups cheddar cheese, shredded
- 4 eggs
- 1 cup milk
- ¼ teaspoon pepper
- ¼ teaspoon garlic powder
- ¼ teaspoon onion powder
- ½ teaspoon salt

Directions

1. In the large skillet cook sausages until no longer pink. Drain fat.
2. Add shredded hash browns to the skillet and cook until lightly brown.
3. Place hash browns in the bottom of oven proof pan, lightly greased. Top with sausages and cheese.
4. It the bowl whisk together eggs, salt, pepper, garlic powder, onion powder, and milk.
5. Pour egg mixture over the hash browns.
6. Preheat the Air Fryer to 350-370 F
7. Place the pan in the fryer into the fryer and cook for 25-30 minutes, until become ready.

Healthy Breakfast

Prep time: 5 minutes, cook time: 10 minutes, serves: 2

Ingredients

- 4 large eggs
- 1 teaspoon mustard
- 2 tablespoon mayonnaise
- 2 tablespoon chopped green onion
- ½ teaspoon smoked paprika
- A pinch of salt and black pepper

Directions

1. Mix together eggs, mustard, mayo, and chopped green onion.
2. Season with salt, pepper, and paprika.
3. Pour the mixture in the baking tray which fits to your air fryer.
4. Cook for 10 minutes at 370 F.

Air Fried Breakfast Eggs

Prep time: 4 minutes, cook time: 15 minutes, serves: 2

Ingredients

- 4 large eggs, beaten
- 2 thin slices ham
- 2 teaspoon unsalted butter
- 2 tablespoon heavy cream
- 3 tablespoon Parmesan cheese, grated
- ⅛ teaspoon smoked paprika
- 2 sprigs fresh chives, chopped
- A pinch of salt to taste
- ¼ teaspoon black pepper, freshly ground

Directions

1. Butter the Pie Pan and put the ham slices, so that the bottom and sides of the Pie Pan are completely covered. Place the pan into the Air Fryer basket.
2. In the medium mixing bowl combine beaten egg with heavy cream. Season with salt and ground black pepper. Whisk well to combine.
3. Pour egg mixture into the Pie Pan, over the ham, and crack the remaining 3 eggs over top. Season lightly with salt and pepper and sprinkle with grated Parmesan cheese.
4. Preheat the Air Fryer to 310-330 F and cook for about 10-12 minutes.
5. When ready, uncover the Fryer and season the eggs with smoked paprika and chopped chives.
6. Using a spatula, remove the shirred eggs from the Pie Pan, and transfer to a plate. Serve warm.

Sandwich with Prosciutto, Tomato and Herbs

Prep time: 2-3 minutes, cook time: 5 minutes, serves: 2

Ingredients

- 2 slices bread
- 2 slices prosciutto
- 2 slices tomato
- 2 slices mozzarella cheese
- 2 basil leaves
- 1 teaspoon olive oil
- Salt and black pepper for seasoning

Directions

1. Take 2 pieces of bread. Add prosciutto on the top. Add mozzarella cheese.
2. Place the sandwich into the Air Fryer and cook for 5 minutes in 380°F without preheating.
3. Using a spatula remove the sandwich.
4. Drizzle olive oil on top. Season with salt and pepper, add tomato and basil.

Delicious Tomato and Onion Quiche

Prep time: 5 minutes, cook time: 12 minutes, serves: 2

Ingredients

- 2 large eggs
- 1 medium-sized tomato, diced
- 1 small onion, diced
- ¼ cup skimmed milk
- ½ cup Cheddar cheese, shredded
- Salt and black pepper, to taste

Directions

1. Prepare 2 small ovenproof bowls. In another bowl beat eggs. Add tomatoes, onion, cheese, milk, and season with salt and pepper. Stir to combine. Fill two small bowls and set aside.
2. Preheat the air fryer to 340 F. Place bowls with egg mixture to the air fryer and cook for 12-15 minutes until ready. Serve.

Fried Eggs with Carrots and Peas

Prep time: 5 minutes, cook time: 10 minutes, serves: 4

Ingredients

- 1 cup frozen peas
- 2 tablespoons olive oil
- 1 small onion, sliced
- 2 medium carrots, chopped
- Couple garlic cloves, minced
- 2 tablespoons soy sauce
- 4 large eggs

Directions

1. Whisk eggs into a bowl and set aside.
2. Grease round baking tray with the olive oil.
3. Add the peas, carrots, onions.
4. Mix minced garlic cloves with soy sauce. Pour in eggs and place the tray in the air fryer.
5. Cook for 15 minutes in the air fryer on 350 F.
6. When ready, serve and enjoy the meal!

Crispy Breakfast Pies

Prep time: 15 minutes, cook time: 15-20 minutes, serves: 4

Ingredients

- 8 oz frozen dough sheet
- 4 eggs
- 1/3 cup ham, cooked & crushed
- 1/3 cup bacon, cooked chopped
- 1/3 cup cheese, shredded

Directions

1. Preheat your Air Fryer to 380 F
2. On work surface, unroll dough. Unroll to form approximately 13x9-inch rectangle. Cut into 4 equal rectangles (6 1/2x4 1/2 inches), and separate. Place dough rectangles on cookie sheet. Make edges toward center to form 1/2-inch rimmed edge around each rectangle.
3. Carefully break 1 egg in center of each dough rectangle. Top each pie with ham, bacon and cheese.
4. Place pies into the Air Fryer and cook for about 15-20 minutes, until edges of crescent dough are golden brown and egg whites and yolks are cooked.
5. Serve and enjoy delicious and healthy breakfast.

Snacks

Appetizing Fried Cheese

Prep time: 5 minutes, cook time: 15 minutes, serves: 2

Ingredients

- 4 slices of white bread or brioche if you have one
- ¼ cup melted butter
- ½ cup sharp cheddar cheese

Directions

1. Cheese and butter put in two bowls. On the each side of the bread brush the butter, and on two of sides put cheese.
2. Grilled cheese put together with bread and all put in Air fryer at 360°F for 5-7 minutes.

Cheese & Bacon Muffins

Prep time: 8 minutes, cook time: 30 minutes, serves: 4-6

Ingredients

- 1 ½ cup all-purpose flour
- 1 large egg, beaten
- 3-4 large bacon slices
- 1 medium-sized onion, sliced
- ½ cup cheese, shredded
- 2 teaspoon baking powder
- 2 tablespoon vegetable oil
- 1 cup skimmed milk
- 1 teaspoon parsley, dried and crushed
- 1/8 teaspoon black pepper, ground
- A pinch of salt to taste

Directions

1. Preheat the sauté pan over the medium-high heat and cook the bacon. When it's almost done add the onion and cook for couple minutes, until transparent and set aside.
2. Combine parsley, baking powder, all-purpose flour, and grated cheese. Then add milk, vegetable oil, egg and cooked bacon with onion. Mix with the wooden spoon until it becomes a sticky to thick dough.
3. Drain the oil from your bacon and onion and also add to the mixture.
4. Preheat the Air Fryer to 390 F. Spoon the mixture into six medium sized muffin cases and cook in the Air Fryer for 20 minutes. Then, reduce the temperature to 350 F and cook additionally for 8-10 minutes to make sure they are cooked in the center. Work in batches to finish all muffins.

Crunchy Jalapeno Peppers

Prep time: 20 minutes, cook time: 10 minutes, serves: 2

Ingredients

- 2-3 jalapeno peppers, sliced
- 1 oz cheddar cheese
- 1 spring roll wrapper
- 1 tablespoon Egg Beaters

Directions

1. Firstly prepare peppers: cut stem end off, slice lengthwise, trim out all seeds and inner core.
2. Cut cheese into ½ oz strips.
3. Peel off a sheet of spring roll wrapper and cut in half. Cover each half with a half tablespoon of liquid egg mixture.
4. Place a half of jalapeno pepper in one corner of the spring roll wrapper half (egg-brushed side up), then place a strip of cheese and then another half of jalapeno.
5. Roll the pepper and cheese tightly in the spring roll wrapper on the diagonal.
6. Check all sides and glue any loose edges with egg mixture.
7. Preheat the Air Fryer to 370°F
8. Lightly spray each wrapping with cooking spray and put them into the Fryer. Cook for about 10 minutes until they become brown.
9. Serve hot or warm.

Easy and Quick Maple Bacon Knots

Prep time: 3 minutes, cook time: 8 minutes, serves: 3-4

Ingredients

- 1 pound smoked bacon
- ¼ cup maple syrup
- ¼ cup brown sugar
- Freshly ground black pepper

Directions

1. Cut the bacon into strips tie each piece in a loose knot. Place on baking sheet.
2. In the large mixing bowl combine the maple syrup and brown sugar. Dip each knot in this mixture and sprinkle generously with freshly ground black pepper.
3. Preheat the air fryer at 370 F.
4. Work in batches: place one layer of knots in the air fryer basket and cook for 7 minutes, shaking couple times through cooking. Depending thickness of the bacon you may cook for additional 2-3 minutes.
5. Serve warm with any dipping sauce you prefer.

Cheese Cookies

Ingredients for the Dough

- 7 oz Gruyere cheese, grated
- 5 oz margarine
- 4 oz cream
- 5 oz flour
- 1 teaspoon mild paprika powder
- ½ teaspoon salt
- ½ teaspoon baking powder

Ingredients to Finish

- 2 egg yolks
- 1 tablespoon milk
- Poppy seeds
- Cumin seeds
- Pistachio nuts, ground
- White and black sesame seeds

Directions

1. Put the margarine, cheese, salt and paprika in a large mixing bowl. Pour in the cream and stir to combine until smooth.
2. Sift the flour and baking powder over your work surface and make a hollow. Knead the cheese mixture into the flour and baking powder to form a dough.
3. Knead as little as possible to prevent the dough becoming tough.
4. Roll the dough out to 3-4 mm thickness and cut out cookie shapes. Mix the beaten eggs with the milk and brush the cookies. Garnish with poppy seeds or sesame seeds.
5. Preheat the air fryer to 330 F and cook cookies for about 12-15 minutes until ready.

Simply Airfryed Sage & Onion Meaty Balls

Prep time: 4 minutes, cook time: 15 minutes, serves: 2-3

Ingredients

- 5 oz sausage meat
- 1 small onion, peeled and diced
- 1 garlic clove, minced
- 1 teaspoon sage, chopped
- 3 tablespoon breadcrumbs
- Salt & pepper to taste

Directions

1. In the large mixing bowl combine sausage meat, diced onion, sage and garlic. Stir well.
2. From the meat mixture form medium sized balls, approximately 2-inch in diameter and coat them with breadcrumbs.
3. Preheat the Air Fryer to 390 F. Cook meat balls for about 5 minutes, until golden and crispy. Do not overload. If you receive a lot of meat balls just cook them in batches.
4. Serve hot or cold.

Mac'N Cheese Balls

Ingredients

- 2 cups leftover macaroni
- 1 cup Cheddar cheese, shredded
- 3 large eggs
- 1 cup milk
- ½ cup flour
- 1 cup breadcrumbs
- ½ teaspoon salt
- ¼ teaspoon black pepper

Directions

1. In a large bowl combine leftover macaroni and shredded cheese. Set aside.
2. In another bowl place flour, and in other - breadcrumbs. In medium bowl whisk eggs and milk.
3. Using ice-cream scoop, make balls from mac'n cheese mixture and roll them first in a flour, then in eggs mixture and then in breadcrumbs.
4. Preheat the air fryer to 365 F and cook mac'n cheese balls for about 10 minutes, stirring occasionally until cook and crispy.
5. Serve with ketchup or another sauce you prefer.

Baked Sausages

Prep time: 5 minutes, cook time: 30 minutes, serves: 3

Ingredients

- 1 tablespoon olive oil
- 8 small sausages
- 6 oz flour
- 2 large eggs
- 5 skimmed milk
- 4 oz cold water
- 1 garlic clove, minced
- 1 medium onion, sliced
- Salt and ground pepper, to taste

Directions

1. Take an ovenproof dish that fits in your air fryer and sprinkle with the olive oil. Add the flour in large mixing bowl and beat the eggs into it.
2. Gradually add the milk, water, the chopped onion and garlic and season to taste with salt and pepper. Stir to combine.
3. Place sausages in the dish. Pour the batter over the sausages. Preheat the air fryer to 320 F and bake the dish for 30 minutes.
4. Serve and enjoy!

Zucchini with Tuna

Prep time: 15 minutes, cook time: 10 minutes, serves: 4

Ingredients

- 4 corn tortillas
- 1 can (6 oz) drained tuna
- 3 tablespoons softened butter
- 1 cup shredded zucchini, squeezed
- 5 tablespoons mayonnaise
- 2 tablespoons mustard
- 1 cup Cheddar cheese, shredded
- Salt and black pepper, to taste

Directions

1. Spread the tortillas with the softened butter.
2. Preheat the air fryer to 370 F. Transfer tortillas to an air fryer and cook for 2-3 minutes until crispy. Remove and set aside.
3. Meanwhile, in the large bowl combine canned tuna, shredded zucchini, mayonnaise, mustard.
4. In a medium bowl, combine the tuna, zucchini mayonnaise, and mustard. Season with salt and pepper and mix well.
5. Spread the tuna mixture to grilled tortillas and sprinkle with shredded cheese and place to an air fryer. Cook for 3-4 minutes, until cheese melted.
6. Serve and enjoy.

Mac & Cheese with Topping

Prep time: 20 minutes, cook time: 5 minutes, serves: 3

Ingredients

- 3 cups macaroni
- 15 pcs Ritz biscuits
- 2 oz gruyere cheese, grated
- 2 oz butter
- 2 tablespoon plain flour
- 16 oz milk
- 1 clove garlic, minced
- 1 cup pizza cheese mix (Mozzarella, Parmesan, Cheddar)

Directions

1. Crush Ritz biscuits, mix with gruyere cheese and set aside.
2. Cook macaroni until almost ready, drained and also set aside.
3. Melt the butter in the separate bowl on the small fire and fry the garlic until fragrant. Add plain flour. Add milk and stir until mixture thickens and looks like a creamy soup. Add remained gruyere cheese and let it melt in the sauce.
4. Bring this sauce to a simmer and switch off the fire. Add macaroni into the mixture and combine well.
5. Dish into individual ceramic bowls.
6. Spoon with Ritz biscuits mixture over macaroni. Top with pizza cheese mix.
7. Preheat the air fryer to 350°F
8. Place ceramic bowls into the Air Fryer and cook for 5 minutes or until pizza cheese mix becomes golden.
9. Serve warm and enjoy.

Delicious Spiced Chickpeas

Prep time: 5 minutes, cook time: 20 minutes, serves: 2

Ingredients

- 1 can (15 oz) chickpeas, rinsed & drained
- 1 tablespoon olive oil
- 1 teaspoon paprika
- ½ tablespoon cumin
- 1 teaspoon salt
- Pinch of cayenne pepper

Directions

1. In the large bowl mix together the chickpeas, olive oil, paprika, cumin, salt and cayenne pepper.
2. Preheat the Air Fryer to 370-390°F
3. Divide chickpeas mixture in batches and place into the Air Fryer. Cook for 8-10 minutes and shake the basket in the middle of cooking.
4. Transfer prepared chickpeas to a bowl and season with salt to taste.

Mediterranean Crunchy Stromboli

Prep time: 7 minutes, cook time: 15 minutes, serves: 4-5

Ingredients

- 12 oz frozen pizza dough
- 3 cups Cheddar cheese, shredded
- 1 cup Mozzarella cheese, shredded
- 1/3 pound cooked ham, sliced
- 1 large red bell pepper, sliced
- 1 egg yolk
- 2 tablespoons skimmed milk
- Salt and black pepper, to taste

Directions

1. Roll out the dough until ¼ inch thick.
2. Lay sliced ham, cheese and peppers on one side of the dough. Fold the dough over to seal.
3. In the large bowl combine egg yolk and milk. Brush folded Stromboli with this mixture.
4. Preheat the air fryer to 360 F. Place Stromboli the frying basket and cook for about 15 minutes, turning over 5-7 minutes, until crunchy.
5. Carefully serve and enjoy.

Sandwich with Roast Turkey

Prep time: 10 minutes, cook time: 13 minutes, serves: 3

Ingredients

- 10 slices roasted turkey breast
- 6 slices whole-grain bread
- 6 tablespoons coleslaw
- tablespoons salted butter
- 12 slices Cheddar cheese
- 2 teaspoons mustard

Directions

1. Spread the butter on one side of 3 bread slices. Lay bread slices buttered side down, on a cutting board.
2. Place cheese, turkey, coleslaw and mustard on the top of each bread slice.
3. Cover filled bread slices with other bread slices and make sandwiches.
4. Preheat the air fryer to 320 F. Cook sandwiches for 5-7 minutes and then turn to other side. Cook for another 5-6 minutes, then slice and serve hot. Enjoy.

Shrimp Toasts

Prep time: 15 minutes, cook time: 10 minutes, serves 4-5

Ingredients

- ¾ pound raw shrimps, peeled and deveined
- 4-5 white bread slices
- 1 egg white
- 3 garlic cloves, minced
- 2 tablespoons cornstarch
- Salt and black pepper, to taste
- 2 tablespoons olive oil

Directions

1. In a medium bowl combine chopped shrimps, egg white, minced garlic, cornstarch, salt and pepper. Stir to combine.
2. Spread shrimp mixture over bread slices with a knife. Sprinkle each slice with olive oil.
3. Preheat the air fryer to 370 F and place bread slices in the basket.
4. Cook for 10 minutes or less, until crispy and lightly brown. Serve.

Mozzarella Fried Sticks

Prep time: 5 minutes, cook time: 13 minutes, serves: 4

Ingredients

- 1 pound Mozzarella cheese
- 2 large eggs
- ¼ cup skimmed milk
- ½ cup plain flour
- 1 cup breadcrumbs
- A pinch of salt, to taste
- 1 tablespoon olive oil

Directions

1. Cut Mozzarella cheese into 1/2-inch sticks.
2. In three different bowls place flour, breadcrumbs and eggs whisked with milk.
3. Dip each Mozzarella stick in flour, then in egg mixture and then in breadcrumbs.
4. Refrigerate sticks for couple hours.
5. Meanwhile, preheat the air fryer to 380 F and sprinkle frying basket with olive oil.
6. Place Mozzarella sticks to an air fryer and cook for 10-13 minutes, turning once while cooking.
7. Enjoy crispy cheese sticks with any dipping sauce you prefer.

Airfryed Spinach Samosa

Prep time: 30 minutes, cook time: 10 minutes, serves: 3-5

Ingredients

- 1 cup all-purpose flour
- ½ cup spinach puree, boiled and blended
- ¼ cup cooked potatoes
- ¼ cup green peas
- 1 teaspoon chopped coriander leaves
- 2 teaspoon sesame seeds
- 2 tablespoon olive oil
- 1 tablespoon spice mixture (Ajwain, chaat masala, chili powder, garam masala)
- ½ teaspoon baking soda

Directions

1. First, you need to prepare dough. In the large mixing bowl combine flour, baking soda, ajwain, some salt. Mix well. Then, add 1 tablespoon olive oil and spinach puree. Prepare smooth mixture and place it in the refrigerator for 15-20 minutes.
2. Meanwhile, prepare the stuffing of samosa. In the small pan heat 1 tablespoon of olive oil over medium heat. Put peas and potatoes and cook for several minutes. Add spices, sesame seeds and stir evenly.
3. Take the batter from the refrigerator and make small, 1-inch balls. Level them out with the rolling pin. Cut it as half and half. At the edge of the flour sheet and give a cone shape. Fill up the cone of the flour sheet with pre-cooked stuffing. Then close the edge of the flour sheet tightly so that it can't be loosen.
4. Preheat the air fryer at 390 F.
5. Put samosa in the air fryer basket and cook for 8 to 10 minutes.
6. Then serve the hot samosa with sauce and enjoy!

Asparagus Spears Rolled with Bacon

Prep time: 10 minutes, cook time: 9 minutes, serves: 3

Ingredients

- 1 bundle asparagus, 20-25 spears
- 4 slices bacon
- 1 garlic clove, crushed
- ½ tablespoon olive oil
- ½ tablespoon sesame oil
- 1 ½ tablespoon brown sugar
- ½ tablespoon toasted sesame seeds

Directions

1. In a medium bowl combine oils, brown sugar, and crushed garlic.
2. Separate bundle of asparagus into four equal-sized bunches and wrap each in a bacon slice.
3. Cover asparagus bunches with oil mixture.
4. Preheat the Air Fryer to 340-360°F
5. Put bunches into the Fryer and sprinkle with sesame seeds.
6. Cook for approximately 8 minutes.
7. Serve and enjoy.

Asparagus Fries with Parmesan

Prep time: 10 minutes, cook time: 10 minutes, serves: 3

Ingredients

- 15-20 asparagus spears
- ½ cup flour
- 1 egg, beaten
- ½ cup whole grain breadcrumbs
- ½ cup Parmesan cheese, grated

Directions

1. Dip the asparagus spears in the flour and shake off the excess.
2. Then dip them into the beaten egg and then into the breadcrumbs.
3. Preheat the Air Fryer to 390°F
4. Place coated asparagus spears into the Air Fryer basket and cook for 10 minutes.
5. Remove them and sprinkle with grated Parmesan cheese on the top.
6. Cook for another 3-5 minutes until cheese becomes golden brown.

Sweet and Salty Snack

Prep time: 5 minutes, cook time: 10 minutes, serves: 8-10

Ingredients

- 1 cup sesame sticks
- 1 cup pumpkin seeds
- 1 cup granola
- 1 cup cashews
- 1 cup mini pretzel crisps
- ½ cup honey
- 3 tablespoons butter, melted
- 1 teaspoon salt

Directions

1. In the large mixing bowl combine honey, butter, and salt. Stir evenly.
2. In another mixing bowl, combine the sesame sticks, pumpkin seeds, granola, cashews, and pretzel crisps. Pour the honey mixture over the top and toss to combine.
3. Preheat air fryer to 370ºF.
4. Cook the snack mix in several batches - do not overload the fryer. Cook each batch for 10-12 minutes, or until the snack mix is lightly toasted. Shake the basket couple times while cooking process to prevent burning.
5. Transfer the snack mix to a cookie sheet and let it chill. Store in an airtight container.

Do not eat much at once ;)

Roasted Pepper Rolls with Feta

Prep time: 10 minutes, cook time 10 minutes, serves: 3

Ingredients

- 2-3 medium-sized yellow or red peppers, halved
- 4 oz Greek feta cheese, crushed
- 1 green onion, sliced
- 2 tablespoon oregano, chopped

Directions

1. Preheat the Air Fryer to 380°F
2. Place peppers in the cooking basket and turn on the fryer.
3. Roast peppers for 10 minutes until skin will become slightly charred.
4. Halve peppers longways and remove skin and seeds.
5. Prepare filling: combine Greek feta cheese with green onion and oregano.
6. Coat pepper pieces with feta mixture and roll them up, starting from the narrowest end.
7. Fix the rolls with tapas forks and serve.

Green Beans with Pears, Sage and Peanuts

Prep time: 8 minutes, cook time: 20 minutes, serves: 6

Ingredients

- 1 pound 5 oz green beans
- 2 pears, not too ripe
- Fresh sage
- 2 tablespoons peanuts
- 3 ½ fl oz low-fat whipping cream
- 3 ½ fl oz vegetable stock
- 1 tablespoon vegetable oil

Directions

1. Cut off the ends of beans and cut them into stripes.
2. Put green beans with sage into the air fryer, pour a tablespoon of oil and cook for about 10 minutes.
3. Add diced pear and peanuts.
4. Then pour in vegetable stock with low-fat whipping cream
5. Cook for another 10 minutes.

Green Bean Rice balls

Prep time: 10 minutes, cook time: 8-10 minutes, serves: 4

Ingredients

- 1 cup cooked rice
- 2 cans (14.5 oz each) green beans, drained
- ¼ cup mushroom cream soup
- 1 cup Mozzarella cheese
- 2 large eggs
- ½ teaspoon salt
- ¼ teaspoon black pepper
- 2 cups breadcrumbs
- 1 ½ cup all-purpose flour

Directions

1. In the large mixing bowl combine cooked rice, drained green beans, mushroom cream soup, and mozzarella cheese. Season with salt and pepper and stir to combine. Fridge the mixture for about 20-30 minutes.
2. In one bowl place all-purpose flour, in another - beaten eggs, in the third one - breadcrumbs.
3. Using your hand, roll the rice mixture into 2-inch balls and then roll each ball in the flour, eggs, and breadcrumbs.
4. Preheat the air fryer to 370 F and cook rice balls for about 8-10 minutes, until golden and crispy.
5. Serve and enjoy.

Appetizer Garlic Knots

Prep time: 5 minutes, cook time: 12 minutes, serves: 4-5

Ingredients

- 1 pound frozen pizza dough
- 4 garlic cloves, minced
- 1 teaspoon salt
- 1 tablespoon freshly chopped parsley
- 2 tablespoons Parmesan cheese, grated
- 4 tablespoons extra virgin olive oil
- Marinara sauce or ketchup for serving

Directions

1. Roll pizza dough out until 1 - 1/2 inch thick.
2. Cut the dough lengthwise. Make knots rolling the dough between countertop and palm.
3. In the large mixing bowl combine olive oil, grated cheese, salt, minced garlic, chopped parsley. Stir to combine.
4. Preheat the air fryer to 360 F.
5. Dip each knot into the oil mixture and transfer to the air fryer. Cook for 10-12 minutes, stirring occasionally, until ready and crispy.
6. Serve with ketchup or marinara sauce. Enjoy.

Green Beans with Shallots and Almonds

Prep time: 5 minutes, cook time: 25 minutes, serves: 4-5

Ingredients

- 1½ pound French green beans, stems removed
- ½ pound shallots, peeled, stems removed and cut into quarters
- ¼ cup slivered almonds, lightly roasted
- 2 tablespoon olive oil
- 1 tablespoon salt
- ½ teaspoon black pepper, ground

Directions

1. Bring water to a boil over high heat. Once boiling, add the green beans, season with salt and cook for 2 minutes. Remove from the water and drain in a colander.
2. Mix cooked beans with quartered shallots, some additional salt and black pepper and sprinkle with the olive oil. Toss well to coat evenly.
3. Cook bean mixture for 25 minutes at 390 F tossing them twice throughout the cooking process. The green beans should be lightly browned and tender once cooked.
4. Transfer cooked beans to a serving platter.

Brussels Sprouts with Pine Nuts & Raisins in Orange Juice

Prep time: 30 minutes, cook time: 20 minutes, serves: 4

Ingredients

- 1 pound Brussels sprouts
- 2 tablespoon raisins
- Juice and zest of 1 orange
- 2 tablespoon pine nuts, toasted
- 1 tablespoon olive oil

Directions

1. Put sprouts to the boiling water and cook for 4-5 minutes, then plunge in cold water, drain and set aside.
2. Squeeze juice from the orange and soak raisins in it for 15-20 minutes.
3. Preheat the Air fryer to 370 F. Combine sprouts in oil and roast for about 15 minutes.
4. Serve with raisins, pine nuts, and orange zest.

Pepperoni Pizza

Prep time: 5 minutes, cook time: 5 minutes, serves: 3

Ingredients

- 3 cleaned and scooped portabella mushroom caps
- 3 tablespoons tomato sauce
- 3 tablespoons olive oil
- 3 tablespoons shredded mozzarella
- 12 slices pepperoni
- 1 pinch dried Italian seasoning
- 1 pinches salt

Directions

1. In Air fryer heated on 330°F put olive oil and drizzle both sides of mushrooms. Add Italian season and salt, spread with tomato sauce and put the cheese on the top.
2. After a minute put the pepperoni on the top of the pizza (do that outside of the fryer!) and cook for 3-5 minutes.
3. At the end, sprinkle with the Parmesan on the top.

Baked Cheesy Crescents

Prep time: 15 minutes, cook time: 15 minutes, serves: 4-5

Ingredients

- 1 pound ground beef
- 8 oz cream cheese softened
- 2 cans crescent rolls
- Salt and pepper to taste

Directions

1. In the skillet prepare ground beef until becomes ready. Drain fat.
2. In the bowl mix cooked ground beef and cream cheese. Season the mixture with salt and pepper to taste.
3. Separate rolls into triangles. Cut each triangle in half length-wise.
4. Scoop a heaping tablespoon into each roll and roll up.
5. Preheat the Air Fryer into 370 F
6. Bake for 15 minutes until crescents become golden and ready.

Fried Tofu Cubes

Prep time: 10 minutes, cook time: 20 minutes, serves: 2

Ingredients

- 12 oz Low-Fat Tofu
- 2 tablespoon soy sauce
- 2 tablespoon fish sauce
- 1 teaspoon sesame or olive oil
- 1 teaspoon Maggi

Directions

1. Cut tofu into 1 inch cubes, place in the medium bowl and set aside.
2. In the large bowl combine all ingredients and make a marinade.
3. Dip tofu to the marinade for at least 20-30 minutes.
4. Preheat the Air Fryer to 370°F
5. Put marinated tofu cubes and cook for 15 minutes. If you want extra crispy cubes, cook for 20-25 minutes.
6. Serve and enjoy!

Bacon Pieces with Cheese

Prep time: 15 minutes, cook time: 35 minutes, serves: 4

Ingredients for Filling

- 4 tablespoons olive oil
- 1 cup flour
- 2 beaten eggs – that means scrambled and beaten with whisk or fork
- 1 cup breadcrumbs

Ingredients for Pillows

- 1 pound thinly sliced bacon
- 1 pound sharp cheddar cheese

Directions

1. Cheddar cheese cut into small parts, 1-inch each and wrap them in sliced bacon, so the cheese is not visible at all. Put in freezer for 5 minutes, but not more than that, you need just to firm it, not freeze.
2. The air fryer put on 390°F and put cheddar rolled into flavor on the bottom, then overflow with eggs and frost with bread soaked with oil on the top.
3. You can double roll the cheese in flavor and eggs to prevent melting the cheese and running out from the meal.
4. Cook 7-8 minutes, until the meal has a brown color.

Mini-pigs in Blankets

Prep time: 10 minutes, cook time: 10 minutes, serves: 3

Ingredients

- 1 tin (8 oz) mini frankfurters
- 4 oz puff pastry
- 1 tablespoon smooth mustard plus some more for serving

Directions

1. Dry frankfurters with paper towels.
2. Cut the puff pastry into 2x1-inch strips.
3. Spread the stripes with mustard.
4. Preheat the Air Fryer to 370°F
5. Wrap each sausage with pastry stripes.
6. Put them into the fryer and cook for nearly 10 minutes or until they will become golden
7. Serve with mustard for dipping.

Feta Pillows

Prep time: 10 minutes, cook time: 20 minutes: serves: 4

Ingredients

- 1 egg yolk
- 2 tablespoons flat-leafed parsley
- 4 ounces feta cheese
- 1 finely chopped scallion
- 2 finely chopped sheets of frozen pastry, but now defrosted
- 2 tablespoons olive oil
- Ground black pepper to taste

Directions

1. Mix beat egg yolk with feta, scallion, parsley and pepper in a bowl.
2. Each sheet of filo cut into three strips.
3. This pasta put with a spoon in the strip of pastry and make a pillow or triangle.
4. Cook in air fryer at 390°F for 3 minutes and then cook on 360ºF for 2 minutes.

Feta Cheese with Onion and Mushrooms

Prep time: 25 minutes, cook time: 15 minutes, serves: 4

Ingredients

- 4 cups small mushrooms
- 6 eggs
- 1 red onion
- 6 tablespoon crumbled feta cheese
- 2 tbsp. olive oil
- Salt to taste

Directions

1. Onion is usually easy for preparing. Peel the onion, wash mushrooms and clean. Peeled onion and mushrooms cut into ¼ inch slices.
2. Mix onion, oil and mushrooms and heat it under medium flame. Some people are afraid of cooking because they don't know when the meal is ready, but that's not a big problem. Check when it's tender with pork and when you sure that is soft, take from the fryer and put in a dry kitchen towel. Wait until completely cool.
3. Mix 6 eggs and whisk vigorously with a pinch of salt (or to taste) and put into a baking dish coated with light pan spray. Yes, we know, it's hard to say what is "to taste" when you can't try it, but it's always good to not put too much. You can add salt later, even the meal is on the table. On the top of the eggs put mushroom and onion mix, then feta cheese.
4. Put the baking dish into fryer at 330°F for 30 minutes.
5. There is an easy trick to know when the meal is ready. Simply put a knife into the dish and if it's clean when you pull out, the meal is ready. Serve with salad and complete the taste of natural cooking.

Classic Cheeseburger

Prep time: 10 minutes, cook time: 5 minutes, serves: 3

Ingredients

- 1 pound ground beef
- 6 dinner rolls
- 6 slices cheddar cheese
- Salt and pepper to taste

Directions

1. As you expect, first you need to from the burgers from beef. The perfect is into 6 2.5-ounce patties. Put salt and pepper as you like, but not too much.
2. Put in Air fryer (which you preheated to 390°F) burgers and cook for 10 minutes, then remove from the fryer, put the cheese on it and back into the fryer for one minute more. That's it.
3. Now you can enjoy in perfect burgers without fat.

Main Dishes

Risotto with Zucchini and Red Capsicum

Prep time: 10 minutes, cook time: 45 minutes, serves: 4

Ingredients

- 1 ½ teaspoons vegetable spice
- 2 cups water
- 1 tin tomato purée 13 oz
- 1 tablespoon
- 3 medium red capsicum
- 1 large zucchini
- 1/2 cup of rice
- 1 large onion
- 4 garlic cloves

Directions

1. Wash all vegetables.
2. Cut zucchini in cubes, capsicum in 1-inch squares, dice onion, chop garlic.
3. Preheat air fryer to 330°F and heat 1 tablespoon of oil in 2 minutes.
4. Put diced onion and cook for 5 minutes until golden, then put chopped garlic and cook another 3-5 minutes.
5. Combine vegetable spice with water, tomato puree and rice. Cook in air fryer for 10 minutes.
6. Add zucchini and capsicum and some water, cook for 20-25 minutes.
7. You can add extra water depending on the consistency you like.

Cheesy Baked Rice

Prep time: 5 minutes, cook time: 25 minutes, serves: 4

Ingredients

- 2 pack overnight cooked rice
- 1 tablespoon butter
- 4 garlic cloves, minced
- 3 tablespoon broccoli florets
- 1 medium-sized carrot, cubed
- 1 veal sausage, sliced
- 8-10 tablespoon creamy sauce
- 3 tablespoon shredded cheddar cheese
- 2 tablespoon shredded mozzarella cheese
- A pinch of salt to taste

Directions

1. Preheat the Air Fryer to 370 F.
2. Melt butter inside baking pan for about 1-2minutes. Sauté minced garlic for about 1-2 minutes or until fragrant. Then add in broccoli florets and carrot cubes and fry for 3-4 minutes. Add a little water will help to speed up the softening.
3. Add sausage slices and cook for 2-3 minutes or until they turn slightly browned. Add in the rice and mix well. Pour in the enough creamy sauce and mix well, level the rice with a ladle.
4. Sprinkle cheese evenly and air fry for 8 - 10 minutes.

Mozzarella Patties Stuffed with Pepperoni

Prep time: 10 minutes, cook time: 8 minutes, serves: 6

Ingredients

- 1 pound Mozzarella cheese
- 20 slices pepperoni
- 2 large eggs
- 1 tablespoon Italian seasoning
- 1 cup all-purpose flour
- 2 cups breadcrumbs
- Salt and black pepper, to taste

Directions

1. Slice Mozzarella cheese into ¼ inch slices and cut each slice in half.
2. Create cheese sandwiches with Mozzarella halves and pepperoni inside. Press to seal.
3. In three different bowls place beaten eggs, breadcrumbs with Italian seasoning, and flour. Dip each cheese sandwich into flour, then into eggs and then into breadcrumb mixture.
4. Preheat the air fryer to 390 F and cook cheese patties for about 6-8 minutes, turning once while cooking.
5. Serve with dipping sauce and enjoy.

Chicken with Delicious Sauce, Vegetables and Rice

Prep time: 10 minutes, cook time: 15 minutes, serves: 4

Ingredients

- 1 pound chicken breasts, skinless and boneless
- ½ pound button mushrooms, sliced
- 1 medium-sized onion, chopped
- 1 package (10 oz) Alfredo sauce
- 2 cups cooked rice
- ½ teaspoon dried thyme
- 1 tablespoon olive oil
- Salt and black pepper, to taste

Directions

1. Slice mushrooms, cut chicken breast into 1-inch cubes, chop onions. Mix ingredients in the large bowl, season with salt and dried thyme, combine well.
2. Preheat the air fryer to 370 F and sprinkle the basket with olive oil. Transfer chicken with vegetables to the fryer and cook to 10-12 minutes, stirring occasionally until cooked and crispy.
3. Open the air fryer and stir in Alfredo sauce. Cook for another 3-4 minutes.
4. Serve cooked meat mixture over cooked rice and enjoy.

Quick Pita Bread Cheese Pizza

Prep time: 5 minutes, cook time: 6 minutes, serves: 4

Ingredients

- 1 piece Pita bread
- ½ pound Mozzarella cheese
- 1 tablespoon olive oil
- 2 tablespoons ketchup
- 1/3 cup sausage
- 1 teaspoon garlic powder

Directions

1. Using a tablespoon spread ketchup over Pita bread. Then, add sausage and cheese. Sprinkle with garlic powder and with 1 tablespoon olive oil.
2. Preheat the air fryer to 340 F and carefully transfer your pizza to a fryer basket.
3. Cook for 6 minutes and enjoy your quick & easy pizza!

Courgette Stuffed with Ground Meat

Prep time: 15 minutes, cook time: 20 minutes, serves: 4

Ingredients

- 1 large courgette
- 2 oz feta cheese, crumbled
- 1 garlic clove, crushed
- 1 teaspoon paprika powder
- ½ pound lean ground beef
- Freshly ground black pepper and salt, to taste

Directions

1. Trim the ends off the courgette and cut it into six equal parts. Set the parts upright and carve them out with a teaspoon to 1/4 inch off the sides and 1/2 inch off the bottom. Sprinkle with salt.
2. Preheat the air fryer to 360 F.
3. Mix the ground beef with the feta cheese, garlic, paprika powder and pepper. Stir to combine. Divide the ground beef into six equal portions and fill the hollow courgette parts with meat mixture. Smooth the top with a moist hand. Put the courgette in the air fryer and cook for 15-20 minutes, until brown and ready.

Noodles with Chicken, Glasswort and Shiitake Mushrooms

Prep time: 10 minutes, cook time: 15 minutes, serves: 3

Ingredients

- 15 oz Udon noodles
- 1 pound chicken fillet
- 4 tablespoons soy sauce
- 1 tablespoon sesame seeds
- 1 teaspoon sambal
- 1 medium-sized onion
- 2 garlic cloves
- 2 tablespoons sesame oil
- ½ cup Shiitake mushrooms
- ½ cup chestnut mushrooms
- ½ cup glasswort
- ½ cup bean sprouts

Directions

1. Cut the chicken into pieces and add to a large mixing bowl. Add soy sauce, sambal and garlic. Stir to combine and let the meat to marinade.
2. Prepare the noodles according to the packaging and drain. Then mix with one tablespoon of sesame oil.
3. Preheat the air fryer to 380 F. Cook the chicken for 6 minutes stirring couple times. Add mushrooms, chopped onion, bean sprouts and glasswort and cook for 5 minutes more. When almost done, add cooked noodles and cook for 3-5 minutes.
4. Sprinkle with sesame seeds and serve.

Hearty Sausage with Sauerkraut

Prep time: 15 minutes, cook time: 40 minutes, serves: 4

Ingredients

- 1 pound link sausages (bratwurst, Italian sweet, turkey, your favorite)
- 2 cans (15oz) sauerkraut, drained
- 1 apple
- 1 onion
- 2 tablespoons diced red sweet pepper
- 1/2 teaspoon caraway seeds
- 2 teaspoons brown sugar
- Couple tablespoons oil for your choice

Directions

1. Cut sausage into 1-inch pieces, put into air fryer drizzle with oil and cook for 20 minutes.
2. Remove sausages and wipe out oil with paper towel.
3. Pour in apple cored and diced into 1-inch cubes, onion diced into 1-inch pieces, red pepper, caraway seeds along with 1 tablespoon of oil. Cook for 10 minutes.
4. Add sauerkraut evenly over apple mixture.
5. Sprinkle brown sugar evenly over sauerkraut.
6. Add sausages back into air fryer and cook for 10 minutes.

Bubble & Squeak

Prep time: 3 minutes, cook time: 23 minutes, serves: 3-4

Ingredients

- Different leftover veggies (potato, sprouts, cabbage, etc)
- 1 medium onion, sliced
- 2 large eggs, beaten
- 3-4 slices turkey or chicken breast
- 2 oz cheddar cheese, grated
- 1 tablespoon mixed herbs or Italian seasoning
- 1teaspoon dried tarragon
- Salt and pepper to taste

Directions

1. Brake up your leftovers in the bowl. Add sliced onion and cheese, beat the eggs and season with herbs and salt.
2. Chop up the turkey and add it to the bowl and mix everything well with your hands or wooden spoon.
3. Preheat the Air Fryer to 370-380 F. Place the mixture into a baking dish and then place in the Air Fryer. Cook for 20-23 minutes until it is bubbling on top.
4. Sprinkle additionally with grated cheese and serve hot.

Pesto Gnocchi

Prep time: 5 minutes, cook time 20 minutes, serves 4

Ingredients

- 1 package (16-ounce) shelf-stable gnocchi
- 1 medium-sized onion, chopped
- 3 garlic cloves, minced
- 1 jar (8 ounce) pesto
- 1/3 cup Parmesan cheese, grated
- 1 tablespoon extra virgin olive oil
- Salt and black pepper, to taste

Directions

1. In the large mixing bowl combine onion, garlic, and gnocchi and sprinkle with the olive oil. Stir to combine.
2. Preheat the air fryer to 340 F. Cook for 15-20 minutes, stirring couple time while cooking, until gnocchi are lightly browned and crisp.
3. Stir in the pesto and Parmesan cheese, and serve immediately.

Arancini with Jerked Tomatoes & Mozzarella

Prep time: 10 minutes, cook time: 10-15 minutes, serves: 5-6

Ingredients

- 1 cup Arborio rice, cooked
- ½ small onion, chopped
- 2 large eggs
- 3 oz Mozzarella cheese
- ⅓ cup Parmigiano-Reggiano cheese, grated
- ¼ cup oil-packed jerked tomatoes, chopped
- 1½ cups Italian seasoned breadcrumbs
- 1 tablespoon olive oil
- Salt and ground black pepper
- Marinara sauce for garnish

Directions

1. In the large mixing bowl combine warm cooker Arborio rice and Parmigiano-Reggiano cheese. Season with salt and pepper. Then, spread the rice mixture out onto a baking sheet to chill.
2. Meanwhile, cut the Mozzarella into ¾-inch cubes.
3. When the rice has chilled, combine it with beaten eggs, jerked tomatoes and ½ cup of the breadcrumbs. The remaining breadcrumbs place in a plate.
4. Shape the rice into 10-12 equal balls. Make a hole in the center of a rice ball with your finger and push one or two cubes of Mozzarella cheese into the hole. Mold the rice back into a ball, enclosing the cheese.
5. Roll the finished rice balls in the breadcrumbs and place them on a baking sheet. Lightly spray the rice balls with olive oil.
6. Preheat the air fryer to 380 F.
7. Working in batches, cook half of the Arancini for 13-15 minutes, turning once while cooking.
8. While you rice balls cook, warm the marinara sauce in a small saucepan.Pool the sauce on the bottom of the serving plate and place the Arancini on the top of the marinara. Enjoy!

Delicious Meatballs

Prep time: 10 minutes, cook time: 20 minutes, serves: 4

Ingredients

- 1 pound 5 oz minced meat (mixture of 60%veal and 40% pork)
- 1 teaspoon ground cumin
- 3 ¼ oz gruyere cheese
- 2 slices white bread
- 3 ½ fl oz milk
- 4-5 sprigs parsley
- 1 egg
- 1 ¾ oz flour

Directions

1. Add minced meat and one bitten egg in the bowl.
2. Soak bread in a warm milk and add it to the meat.
3. Add to the mixture cumin and chopped parsley. Mix vigorously with a fork, season to taste.
4. Roll small meatballs with hands. Stuff each meatball with a small piece of cheese and close meatball up to avoid running cheese out while cooking.
5. Roll meatballs in a flour and cook them in several batches in the air fryer for 20 minutes.

Potato Recipes

French Fries Sprinkled with Parmesan

Prep time: 15 minutes, cook time: 40 minutes, serves: 4

Ingredients

- ½ teaspoon dried thyme
- ½ teaspoon steak spice
- 1 tablespoon olive oil
- a pinch rosemary dried and crumbled
- 2 pounds potatoes cut into "shoestrings"
- Parmesan cheese to taste

Directions

1. Wash potatoes, cut them into nearly ¼ inch x 3-inch stripes and dry them using a paper towel.
2. Preheat your air fryer to 330-350°F.
3. Place potato slices in a cooking basket and add thyme, steak spice, rosemary and sprinkle with oil.
4. Put spiced and oil-coated potato slices to air fryer and cook for 35-40 minutes, until golden and crispy.
5. Plate and grate parmesan profusely over the top.

Crispy Classic French Fries

Prep time: 35 minutes, cook time: 10 minutes, serves: 4

Ingredients

- 6 russet peeled potatoes, medium size
- 2 tablespoon olive oil

Directions

1. After you peeled the potatoes, cut them into small parts, perfect is around ¼ inch by 3-inch strips. First, soak them in water, at least for 30 minutes, and then dry them with a paper towel.
2. The Air fryer should be on 360°F, put the potatoes mixed with oil in it.
3. Cook for 30 minutes, but it can be shorter if the potatoes are soft and in small parts. The perfect is when they have grown brown color. You obviously can short time of cooking if you slice the potatoes on small parts.
4. It's also good if you shake the potatoes during the cooking 2-3 times.

Potatoes with Black Beans

Prep time: 6 minutes, cook time: 15 minutes, serves: 2

Ingredients

- 1 large cooked potato, mashed
- 1 can (15 oz) black beans, drained
- 2 garlic cloves, minced
- 1/3 cup Cheddar cheese, grated
- Salt and pepper, to taste

Directions

1. Make a layer of mashed potato in the round baking dish. Add black beans and garlic. Season with salt and pepper, to taste.
2. Preheat the air fryer to 360 F. Sprinkle potatoes and beans with cheese and place to the air fryer.
3. Cook for 15 minutes and serve hot.

Mashed Potato Tots

Prep time: 15 minutes, cook time: 12-15 minutes, serves: 2

Ingredients

- 1 large potato
- 1 teaspoon onion, minced
- 1 teaspoon oil
- Salt and black pepper to taste

Directions

1. Boil peeled potato over high heat.
2. Once the potato is almost ready remove it from the water. (It needs to be slightly harder than you need for mash)
3. Mash potato and mix with minced onion and oil. Season to taste.
4. Preheat the Air Fryer to 370 F
5. Make tater tots from the potato mixture and cook them in the air fryer for about 7 minutes. Shake once and cook for another 3-5 minutes.

Home Fried Potatoes with Vegetables

Prep time: 30 minutes, cook time: 30 minutes, serves: 4

Ingredients

- 4 medium potatoes, scrubbed and diced into ½ inch cubes
- 1 medium onion, diced
- 2 garlic cloves, minced
- 1 teaspoon smoked paprika
- 1 small red pepper, diced
- 1 small carrot, diced
- 2 tablespoons olive oil
- 1 teaspoon salt
- Ground black pepper to taste
- Freshly chopped parsley for garnish

Directions

1. First, you need to prepare potatoes. Scrub and dice it, and soak in water for 20-30 minutes.
2. Meanwhile, dice onion, carrot, and red pepper.
3. Drain and dry potato cubes and combine them with vegetables in the large bowl. Sprinkle with the olive oil and mix well.
4. In another bowl mix together all seasonings.
5. Preheat the air fryer to 380 F.
6. Place potato mixture into the frying basket and cook for 20-25 minutes, shaking couple time during cooking. Potatoes should be completely cooked and soft.
7. Dump vegetables into the large mixing bowl and cover with prepared seasonings. Mix well. Place the mixture back to the fryer and cook additionally for 5 minutes.
8. Top with fresh parsley, serve hot and enjoy!

Hash browns

Prep time: 5 minutes, cook time: 16 minutes, serves: 3

Ingredients

- 2 cups cubed potatoes
- 2 garlic cloves, minced
- 2 tablespoons of olive oil
- Salt and black pepper, to taste
- Sour cream for serving

Directions

1. Preheat the air fryer to 360 F.
2. Place the cubed potatoes in a bowl and sprinkle with olive oil. Stir to combine.
3. Add minced garlic and season with salt and pepper.
4. Make medium-sized hash browns and place them in the air fryer. Cook for about 13-16 minutes, turning once during cooking, until golden brown.
5. Serve with sour cream.

Amazing Fried Potatoes

Prep time: 15 minutes, cook time: 1 hour 50 minutes, serves: 3

Ingredients

- 2 (15oz) potatoes
- 2 stripes bacon, chopped
- 1/3 cup cheddar cheese
- 1 tablespoon green onion, chopped
- 1 tablespoon butter
- 1 teaspoon olive oil
- A pinch of salt
- Ground black pepper to taste

Directions

1. Preheat the Air Fryer to 370-390°F
2. Rub potatoes with olive oil and cook in the Fryer for 30-50 minutes until it becomes fork tender. Remove potatoes from the Air Fryer and set aside to cool.
3. While potatoes cooks, chop bacon stripes into ½ inch pieces, put in a sauté pan and cook until it becomes crispy and golden, for nearly 10 minutes. Remove cooked bacon and set aside.
4. Take chilled potatoes and cut it in half lengthwise. Using a spoon scoop out potato pulp leaving about 1/4 inch border of potato pulp next to the skin.
5. Add cooked bacon and its fat to the potato pulp, ¼ cup of shredded cheese, 1 ½ teaspoon of green onion, butter, salt, and pepper. Stir to combine.
6. Divide the mixture between potato skins and fill them. Sprinkle potato halves with the remaining cheese.
7. Place potatoes to the Air Fryer basket side by side and cook at 390°F for about 15-20 minutes until cheese melted and becomes golden brown.
8. Once cooked replace potatoes from the Fryer and sprinkle with the remaining green onion.
9. Serve warm.

Fried Potatoes with Mushrooms

Prep time: 5 minutes, cook time: 22-25 minutes, serves: 3

Ingredients

- 5 oz mushrooms
- 5 oz onions, finely chopped
- 1 tablespoon spoon olive oil
- 1 lb 5 oz washed and peeled potatoes

Directions

1. Wash and rinse potatoes well. Then cut potatoes into nearly 1-inch cubes.
2. Wash and cut mushrooms into quarters.
3. Heat the olive oil in the air fryer and cook the finely chopped onion in 2-3 minutes.
4. When the onion starts to become transparent, put potato cubes to the cooking basket.
5. Cook for 10-15 minutes, until potato cubes are nearly cooked.
6. Add mushroom quarters to an air fryer and cook for 2 minutes.

Parmesan Potato Pancakes

Prep time: 5 minutes, cook time: 10 minutes, serves: 3-4

Ingredients

- 2 cups leftover mashed potatoes
- 1 large egg
- 2 tablespoons Parmesan, grated
- 2 tablespoons green onions, chopped
- ¼ cup seasoned breadcrumbs, divided
- 2 tablespoons olive oil, divided
- Salt and black pepper, to taste

Directions

1. In a large mixing bowl combine eggs, mashed potatoes, 2 tablespoons breadcrumbs and green onions. Stir to combine.
2. In the large plate mix grated cheese and 2 tablespoons breadcrumbs
3. Line the basket of your air fryer with parchment and coat with oil. Shape the potato mixture into 8 patties and coat with breadcrumb mixture.
4. Preheat the air fryer to 350 F, place pancakes to the fryer and cook for about 10 minutes, turning once.
5. Serve and enjoy!

Potato Halves with Bacon and Herbs

Prep time: 5 minutes, cook time: 30 minutes, serves: 4

Ingredients

- 4 middle-sized potatoes, peeled and halved
- 6 garlic cloves, minced
- 4 slices bacon, cut into 1-inch pieces
- 2 sprigs rosemary, crushed
- 1 tablespoon olive oil
- ¼ teaspoon black pepper, freshly ground
- A pinch of salt

Directions

1. Preheat your Air fryer to 370 F.
2. Combine halved potatoes, minced garlic, rosemary, and bacon pieces. Sprinkle the mixture with olive oil, season with salt and pepper. Mix well.
3. Put everything in the air fryer basket and cook for 25-30 minutes, or until golden brown.

Cheesy Hasselback Potatoes

Prep time: 10 minutes, cook time: 45 minutes, serves: 3

Ingredients

- 10 medium sized potatoes
- 4 oz cheese, sliced
- 3 tablespoons olive oil
- 1 tablespoon fresh chives, chopped
- Salt and ground pepper to taste

Directions

1. Wash and dry potatoes with paper towels.
2. Cut potatoes thinly as shown on the picture.
3. Sprinkle with olive oil.
4. Season with ground pepper and salt to taste.
5. Preheat the Air Fryer to 360°F
6. Place potatoes to the fryer and bake for 30-35 minutes.
7. Insert cheese slices into each potato and sprinkle with chopped fresh chives.
8. Cook for another 3-5 minute until cheese becomes golden.
9. Serve with sour cream.

Potato Chips

Prep time: 5 minutes, cook time: 22 minutes, serves: 2

Ingredients

- 2 large russet potatoes
- ½ tablespoon extra virgin olive oil
- Salt to taste

Directions

1. Peel and slice the potatoes thinly.
2. Soak slices in a bowl of cold water for 30 minutes; change the water halfway through and give the slices a good mix.
3. Cook potato slices for about 20 minutes at 390 F.
4. When ready, replace chips in the large plate, season with salt to taste and serve.

Cheesy Potatoes

Prep time: 7 minutes, cook time: 25 minutes, serves: 4

Ingredients

- 2 pounds potatoes, cut into strips
- 1/2 teaspoon dried thyme
- A pinch rosemary dried and crumbled
- 1 tablespoon olive oil
- ½ cup grated parmesan

Directions

1. Cut potatoes into nearly ¼ inch x 3-inch stripes and dry them using a paper towel.
2. Preheat your air fryer to 330-350°F.
3. Sprinkle potatoes with olive oil, thyme, and rosemary.
4. Cook in the air fryer for 20-25 minutes, until golden and crispy.
5. Serve and top with grated parmesan.

Potatoes with Garlic, Tomatoes and Shrimps

Prep time: 8 minutes, cooking time: 35 minutes, serves: 4

Ingredients

- 1 pound 12 oz small new potatoes, unpeeled
- 4 peeled, seeded and chopped tomatoes
- 12 raw prawns or large shrimp, peeled
- 2 tablespoons of finely chopped parsley or fresh Provence herbs
- 2 heads garlic
- 2 tablespoons of olive oil
- salt and freshly ground pepper for seasoning

Directions

1. Wash potatoes and dry them with a paper towel.
2. Separate garlic cloves without removing the peel. Wash and dry them.
3. Put potatoes and garlic in the air fryer and cook for 15-20 minutes.
4. Add unpeeled tomatoes to the air fryer and cook for another 10 minutes.
5. Add the shrimps and herbs. Cook for 5 minutes or until shrimps will be ready.

Potatoes with Garlic and Coriander

Prep time: 6 minutes, cook time: 40 minutes, serves: 3

Ingredients

- 2 tablespoons of fresh coriander leaves finely chopped
- 2 fresh garlic cloves finely chopped
- 1 tablespoon of olive oil
- 1 tablespoon vegetable oil
- 1 lb 12 oz peeled, washed potatoes
- Salt to taste

Directions

1. Wash and rinse potatoes well. Cut them into cubes and dry with paper towel carefully.
2. Mix olive oil, coriander and fresh finely chopped garlic in a small bowl and set aside.
3. Preheat air fryer to 330°F.
4. Put potato cubes into your air fryer and pour the vegetable oil evenly over the potatoes.
5. Cook for 35 minutes.
6. Add the olive oil with coriander and garlic and cook additionally for 5 minutes.
7. Season to taste with salt.

Tender Potato Pillows

Prep time: 15 minutes, cook time: 30 minutes, serves: 4

Ingredients for Filling

- 4 peeled and cubed russet potatoes, medium size
- 1 cup parmesan cheese,
- 2 egg yolks,
- 2 tablespoons grated all-purpose flour
- 1 pinches salt
- 3 tablespoons finely chopped chives
- 1 pinches nutmeg

Ingredients for Breading

- 2 beaten eggs
- 3 tablespoons vegetable oil
- ¾ cup all-purpose flour
- ¾ breadcrumbs

Directions

1. First, potatoes should be boiled. Cook it in the water for 15 minutes and then drain it with a paper towel. Then mash them in a large bowl.
2. In other bowl mix cheese, egg yolk, chives, and flour. Add salt, nutmeg and pepper. Roll small balls between the hands in the size of golf balls.
3. Mix breadcrumbs with oil and each potato ball roll in that mixture. Then place in the eggs and finally in the flour.
4. Cook in the air fryer on 390°F for 7-8 minutes or until balls become golden brown.

Incredible Cheesy Bacon Fries

Prep time: 10 minutes, cook time: 30 minutes, serves: 4-5

Ingredients

- 3 medium-sized russet potatoes
- 6 slices of bacon, chopped
- 2 cups Cheddar cheese, shredded
- 3 oz cream cheese, melted
- ¼ cup chopped scallions
- 2 tablespoon olive oil
- Salt and freshly ground black pepper to taste

Directions

1. At first, you need to bring a large pot of salted water to a boil over high heat. Meanwhile, peel the potatoes and cut them into 1/2 - inch sticks. Blanch the potatoes in the boiling water for 4 minutes. Strain the potatoes in a colander and rinse them with cold water to wash off the starch. Dry potatoes with a kitchen towel.
2. Preheat the air fryer to 380 F.
3. Chop the bacon and place into the air fryer. Cook for 4 minutes, shaking occasionally through the cooking process. Remove cooked bacon on the paper towel to remove the fat and discard the grease from the bottom of the air fryer drawer.
4. Sprinkle potato sticks with olive oil and place in the air fryer basket. Cook at 350 F for 20 minutes, shaking couple times while cooking. Season potatoes with salt and ground pepper through cooking.
5. When cooked, transfer your fries from the air fryer to a casserole dish which fits your air fryer basket. Combine with 2 cups of shredded Cheddar cheese and melted cream cheese. Top the mixture with cooked bacon crumbles.
6. Place the casserole dish into the air fryer basket and cook for 5 minutes, until cheese melted.
7. Sprinkle the fries with chopped scallions and serve.

Potato with Crispy Skin

Prep time: 20 minutes, cook time: 40 minutes, serves: 5

Ingredients

- 6 potatoes (medium size)
- 2 tbsp. canola oil
- 1 ½ teaspoon paprika
- Salt and pepper to taste

Directions

1. Clean potato under the cold and running water. Put it in salted water. Boil potatoes for 40 minutes and when you sure that they are tender, cool in a refrigerator for 30 minutes.
2. Mix paprika and canola oil. Add salt and pepper to taste. Paprika is the spice which will make your potato red and crispy.
3. Potatoes cut into quarters or medium cubes and mix with the oil and spices.
4. Put into the fryer, be careful to not overcrowd. Fryer can't work if it's too loaded, and it can be dangerous.
5. Cook the potatoes for 14-16 minutes on the 390°F. You'll recognize when it's finished, potatoes should be golden brown with crispy skin.

Spicy Potato Wedges

Preparation time: 40 minutes, cook time: 20 minutes, serves: 2

Ingredients

- 1 pound potatoes
- 1 tablespoon olive oil
- 1 tablespoon Provencal herbs
- Salt to taste

Directions

1. Cut potatoes into equal-sized wedges.
2. Fill the large bowl with cold water and dip potato widgets for 30 minutes.
3. Dry potatoes with paper towels.
4. Place dried widgets into another bowl and evenly sprinkle the potatoes with Provencal herbs, olive oil, and salt.
5. Preheat the Air Fryer to 370°F
6. Put covered potato wedges to the Fryer basket and cook for 15 minutes or until become ready and golden.
7. Serve with sour cream.

Crispy and Tasty Garlic-Parsley Potatoes

Prep time: 7 minutes, cook time: 25-30 minutes, serves: 3-4

Ingredients

- 1 pound Russet baking potatoes
- 1 tablespoon garlic powder
- 1 tablespoon freshly chopped parsley
- ½ teaspoon salt
- ¼ teaspoon black pepper
- 1-2 tablespoons olive oil

Directions

1. Wash and dry potatoes with kitchen towels. Make holes in each potato with a fork.
2. Transfer potatoes to a large bowl and sprinkle with garlic powder, salt and pepper. Drizzle with the olive oil and stir to combine.
3. Preheat the air fryer to 360 F. Cook potatoes for about 30 minutes, shaking couple times during cooking.
4. When ready sprinkle potatoes with chopped parsley and serve. You may also serve with butter, sour cream or another dipping you prefer.

Amazing Potato Bites with Cheese

Prep time: 20 minutes, cook time: 25 minutes, serves: 2

Ingredients

- 2 large Russet potatoes, peeled and cut
- ½ cup parmesan cheese, grated
- ½ cup breadcrumbs
- 2 tablespoon all-purpose flour
- ¼ teaspoon nutmeg, ground
- 2 tablespoon fresh chives, finely chopped
- 1 egg yolk
- 2 tablespoon olive oil
- ¼ teaspoon black pepper, ground
- Salt to taste

Directions

1. In lightly salted water boil potato cubes for about 15 minutes.
2. Drain potatoes and mash them finely with the potato masher. Let them completely cool.
3. To the mashed potato add egg yolk, grated cheese, chives, and flour.
4. Season the mixture with ground pepper, nutmeg, and salt.
5. Make 1 ½ inch balls and place them in the flour and then to the breadcrumbs.
6. Preheat the Air Fryer to 370-390°F
7. Carefully place handmade potato rolls to the Air Fryer basket and cook for about 10 minutes, until they become golden brown.
8. Serve either warm or cold and enjoy!

Vegetable Recipes

Mediterranean Vegetable Stir-Fry

Prep time: 10 minutes, cook time: 25 minutes, serves: 4

Ingredients

- 1 zucchini 7 oz
- 5 ¼ oz white mushrooms
- 1 medium aubergine (eggplant)
- 1 red pepper
- 1 green pepper
- 3 1/2 fl oz dry white wine
- 2 tablespoons spoon crushed cloves garlic
- Few sprigs of parsley for decoration
- 2 tablespoons olive oil
- Salt and pepper to taste

Directions

1. Wash vegetables. Dry them with a paper towel.
2. Cut zucchini and aubergine into slices. Do not peel them. Strew with salt and paper and set aside for about 15 minutes. After 15 minutes cut them into cubes.
3. Clean and slice mushrooms.
4. Clean and cut peppers into stripes.
5. Put zucchini, aubergine, mushrooms and peppers into your air fryer, pour in the oil and cook for 15 minutes.
6. Crush the garlic.
7. Add garlic and white wine into the air fryer. Cook for about 10 minutes.
8. Season, décor with parsley.

Cauliflower Buffalo Bites

Prep time: 5 minutes, cook time: 20 minutes, serves: 3

Ingredients

- 1 large head cauliflower, cut into florets
- 1 tablespoon olive oil
- 2 teaspoon garlic powder
- ½ cup Buffalo Style sauce or other hot sauce for your choice
- 1 tablespoon melted butter
- ¼ teaspoon salt
- ¼ teaspoon ground pepper

Directions

1. Cut cauliflower into bite-sized florets.
2. Place cauliflower florets into large plastic bag add olive oil, garlic powder, salt, and pepper. Close bag and toss ingredients and make sure all florets coated.
3. Preheat the Air Fryer to 400°F
4. Place coated florets to the cooking basket and cook for 15 minutes, turning once during cooking.
5. Remove cauliflower from the fryer.
6. Melt the butter and add the hot sauce. Toss florets and cover all of them with this mixture.
7. Return to the Air Fryer and cook for another 5 minutes.
8. Serve warm with any sauce you prefer, for example, blue cheese dip or sour cream.

Cheesy Courgette Gratin

Prep time: 12 minutes, cook time: 15 minutes, serves: 4

Ingredients

- 2 medium courgettes
- 1 tablespoon fresh parsley, chopped
- 1 tablespoons breadcrumbs
- 4 oz cheese, grated
- 1 tablespoon olive oil
- Salt and ground pepper to taste

Directions

1. Cut every courgette in half lengthways and then cut each piece in a half one more time. You need to get 8 pieces from each courgette.
2. In a large bowl combine parsley, breadcrumbs, cheese, olive oil, ground pepper and salt.
3. Preheat the Air Fryer to 370°F
4. Place courgette pieces into the Air Fryer. Top them with the mixture from the bowl.
5. Cook for 15 minutes or until courgette gratin will become ready and golden.
6. You may serve either cold or warm with your favorite sauce.

Veggie Falafel

Prep time: 10 minutes, cook time: 15 minutes, serves: 4

Ingredients

- 2 small potatoes, grated
- 2 carrots, grated
- 2 tablespoons vegetable or olive oil
- 1 green chili, chopped
- Fresh coriander, chopped
- 1 egg
- 1 cabbage, shredded
- Half of papaya, grated
- 2 tablespoon almond flour
- Salt to taste
- ½ teaspoon baking soda
- 1 large onion, diced
- ¼ cup chopped cilantro

Directions

1. Preheat the air fryer to 320 F.
2. Whisk the egg in a bowl. Add all ingredients to the bowl. Stir to combine well and create round or flat falafel.
3. Add the oil to your air fryer. Add the falafel and cook for about 10 minutes.

Sweet Potato Fries with Curry

Prep time: 5 minutes, cook time: 10 minutes, serves: 3

Ingredients

- 1 pound frozen sweet potato fries
- ½ cup sour cream
- ½ cup mango chutney
- 3 teaspoons curry powder, divided
- 1 tablespoon olive oil
- ½ teaspoon salt
- ¼ teaspoon black pepper

Directions

1. In the large mixing bowl combine sour cream, mango chutney, salt, pepper, and 1/2 curry powder. Mix well.
2. In another large bowl place frozen sweet potato fries. Sprinkle with olive oil and 1/2 of curry powder. Stir to combine.
3. Preheat the air fryer to 380 F and cook potato fries for nearly 10 minutes, until cooked and crispy. Shake the fryer basket couple times during cooking.
4. Serve sweet fries with dipping sauce and enjoy.

Air Fried Corn

Prep time: 5 minutes, cook time: 10 minutes, serves: 3-4

Ingredients

- 4 fresh ears corn
- 2 teaspoons extra virgin olive oil
- Salt and pepper, to taste

Directions

1. Remove and discard husks from corn, wash and pat dry. Cut corn in 4-5 inch pieces and transfer to a large bowl.
2. Sprinkle corn with olive oil and season with salt and pepper, to taste.
3. Preheat the air fryer to 390 F. Cook corn for about 8-10 minutes, shake couple times during cooking.
4. Serve.

Lemony Green Beans

Prep time: 2 minutes, cook time: 10-12 minutes, serves: 4

Ingredients

- 1 pound green beans, washed and destemmed
- 1 middle-sized lemon
- ¼ teaspoon black pepper to taste
- 1 teaspoon oil
- A pinch of salt

Directions

1. Prepare green beans: wash them, dry with kitchen towels and cut stems.
2. Preheat the Air Fryer to 390 F. Put green beans in the Air Fryer and add a few squeezes of lemon. Season with salt and ground pepper and drizzle oil over top.
3. Cook in the Air Fryer for 10-12 minutes and serve hot.

Onion Rings

Prep time: 6 minutes, cook time: 10 minutes, serves: 2

Ingredients

- 1 large onion, cut into 1/4 inch slices
- 1 cup all purpose flour
- 1 teaspoon baking powder
- 1 egg, beaten
- 1 cup skimmed milk
- ¾ cup bread crumbs
- 1 teaspoon salt

Directions

1. Preheat the Air Fryer to 360 F.
2. Separate onion slices into rings.
3. Stir together flour, baking powder and salt.
4. Dip onion rings into flour mixture until they are all coated. Set aside.
5. Whisk egg and milk into flour using a fork. Dip the floured onion rings into the batter to coat.
6. Spread bread crumbs on a plate or shallow dish and dredge the rings into the crumbs, making sure it's all covered.
7. Place all the onion rings into Air Fryer and cook for 7-10 minutes until a little dark.

Spicy Grilled Tomatoes

Prep time: 5 minutes, cook time: 20 minutes, serves: 2

Ingredients

- 2 medium tomatoes, sliced
- Herbs you like (I prefer Provencal herbs but it can be parsley, oregano, basil, thyme, rosemary or something else)
- Ground pepper and salt to taste
- 1 tablespoon olive oil or cooking spray

Directions

1. Wash tomatoes, dry them with paper kitchen towels.
2. Cut them in half. Turn halves cut side up. Sprinkle tops with olive oil or cooking spray. Season with ground pepper and herbs dried or fresh.
3. Set your Air Fryer to 320 °F (without preheating), place tomato halves and cook for 20 minutes. Depending on tomatoes size, how many halves you prepare and your personal preference preparation time can vary.

Tip: you can serve grilled tomatoes piping hot, room temperature or chilled.

Fried Vegetables – Winter Combination

Prep time: 15 minutes, cook time: 10 minutes, serves: 4

Ingredients

- 1 small cup pumpkin (1 1/3 cup)
- 1 small cup parsnips (1 1/3 cup)
- 2 red onions
- 1 tablespoons fresh thyme needles
- 3-4 stalks celery (1 1/3 cup)
- 1 tablespoon olive oil
- Pepper and salt to taste

Directions

1. First, you need to prepare the vegetables. That will short your time for preparing and it is easy - wash them, then peel onion and parsnips. Celery and parsnips cut into 2 cm cubes. Cut onion into wedges and pumpkin into cubes. Put all in the fryer.
2. Add olive oil and thyme, pepper and salt add to taste. Try to not put too much of salt.
3. Fry on the temperature 390°C for 20 minutes.
4. Stir the meal only once during the frying. That'll prevent sticking on the pan.
5. Again, don't worry if you don't know how to recognize when is it finished, the vegetables should be brown when it's done.

Vegetable Lasagna

Prep time: 10 minutes, cook time: 25 minutes, serves: 4

Ingredients for the Filling

- 3/4 cup ricotta
- 1/3 cup red bell pepper, chopped
- 2 cups baby spinach, chopped
- ½ cup grated Parmesan cheese
- 3 garlic cloves, chopped
- 1 teaspoon olive oil
- 4 large basil leaves
- 1 large onion, chopped
- 1 large egg
- Salt to taste

Ingredients for the Marinara

- 1 teaspoon olive oil
- 1 garlic clove, minced
- 1 tbsp chopped basil
- 1 ½ cups crushed tomatoes
- Salt and black pepper
- Ingredients for the Zucchini Boats
- 4 medium zucchini
- 1 cup mozzarella, shredded

Directions

1. Preheat the air fryer to 400 F. Sprinkle some olive oil and add the onion, red pepper, garlic and a pinch of salt. Cook for 1 minute and then add the baby spinach. Season with salt. Mix well and transfer to a plate.
2. Combine cheese and egg together in a large mixing bowl. Stir to combine and add the marinara ingredients, basil and the baby spinach mixture. Mix well and set aside. Prepare zucchini by cutting it in halves. Take out the inside of the zucchini and fill it using the cheese mixture. Add them to the zucchini halves.
3. Transfer to the air fryer and cook for 20 minutes.
4. Serve and enjoy.

Rice and Vegetable Stuffed Tomatoes

Prep time: 12 minutes, cook time 25 minutes, serves: 3

Ingredients

- 3 tomatoes, cored
- 2 cups white rice, cooked
- 1 medium onion, diced
- 1 medium carrot, diced
- 1 tablespoon Olive oil
- 1 clove garlic, minced
- Ground pepper
- Salt, to taste

Directions

1. Sprinkle the olive oil in a skillet and sauté carrot, onion, and garlic for 2-3 minutes, season the mixture with salt and pepper.
2. Add cooked rice to the vegetable mixture, stir to combine.
3. Preheat the Air Fryer to 340°F.
4. Fill in cored tomatoes with mixture.
5. Place stuffed tomatoes into the air fryer and cook for 20-25 minutes.
6. Serve warm and enjoy.

Juicy Ratatouille

Prep time: 10 minutes, cook time: 15 minutes, serves:4

Ingredients

- 1 medium courgette or aubergine at your choice, cubed
- 2 yellow or red medium peppers, cubed
- 3 large tomatoes, cubed
- 2 small onions, cubed
- 3 garlic cloves, minced
- 2 tablespoons Provencal herbs
- 1 tablespoon olive oil
- 1 tablespoon vinegar
- Salt and pepper to taste

Directions

1. Wash all vegetables and dry them with paper towels.
2. Cut peppers, tomatoes, onions, courgette or aubergine into 1-inch cubes.
3. In the large bowl place all vegetables, add minced garlic and Provencal herbs. Season with salt and pepper to taste.
4. Stir in olive oil and vinegar.
5. Preheat the Air Fryer to 360°F
6. Put vegetable mixture into the ovenproof dish and place it in the air fryer.
7. Cook for 15 minutes and stir once while preparing.
8. Serve and enjoy.

Broccoli with Cheddar cheese

Prep time: 10 minutes, cook time: 12 minutes, serves: 3

Ingredients

- 1 head broccoli, steamed and chopped
- 1 tablespoon olive oil
- 1 ½ cup Cheddar cheese, grated
- 1 teaspoon salt

Directions

1. Steam the broccoli, cool after that and separate pieces from the stem.
2. In a large bowl combine broccoli florets with grated cheddar cheese.
3. Preheat the Air Fryer to 340-360°F.
4. Place broccoli and cheese mixture to the blender, pulse couple times.
5. Form balls from the mixture with your hands, about 0,5-1 inch in diameter.
6. Place broccoli balls into the Fryer sprinkle with oil and cook for 10-12 minutes.
7. Remove the balls, sprinkle with salt and serve with sour cream, or any sauce you like.

Fried Vegetable Mix (Zucchini, Yellow Squash & Carrots)

Prep time: 10 minutes, cook time: 35 minutes, serves: 3

Ingredients

- ½ pound carrots, peeled
- 1 pound zucchini
- 1 pound yellow squash
- 2-3 tablespoon olive oil
- 1 teaspoon salt
- ½ teaspoon ground white pepper
- 1 tablespoon tarragon leaves, chopped

Directions

1. Cut carrots into 1-inch cubes, mix with 1 tablespoon of olive oil and stir to combine.
2. Preheat the Air Fryer to 390°F
3. Place carrots to the Air Fryer and cook for 5 minutes.
4. While carrots cook, prepare other vegetables. Trim stem and root ends from zucchini and cut into ¾-inch half moons. Also, trim stem and root end from yellow squash and cut into ¾-inch half moons.
5. Place vegetables into large mixing bowl and sprinkle with the remaining olive oil, season with white pepper and salt. Coat all vegetables evenly.
6. Once the time in the Air Fryer goes off, add there zucchini and yellow squash.
7. Cook for another 30 minutes, mixing couple time through the cooking process.
8. When vegetables prepared, remove them and sprinkle with tarragon.
9. Serve warm and enjoy.

Cheesy Fried Broccoli

Prep time: 10-12 minutes, cook time: 25 minutes, serves: 4

Ingredients

- 2 pounds broccoli, cut into florets
- 2 tablespoon olive oil
- 1/3 cup Kalamata olives, pitted and halved
- ½ teaspoon ground black pepper
- 2 teaspoon lemon zest, grated
- 4-6 slices Parmesan cheese
- A pinch of salt

Directions

1. Cook broccoli florets into salted water. Remove from the water drain well and toss with olive oil, salt, and pepper.
2. Preheat the Air Fryer to 370-390°F
3. Place oiled broccoli into the Fryer and cook for 15 minutes, shaking couple times during frying.
4. When the timer goes off, remove cooked broccoli and transfer to the serving bowl.
5. Toss with halved olives, lemon zest, and Parmesan slices and serve.

Oil-Free Fried Broccoli

Prep time: 40 minutes, cook time: 10 minutes, serves: 3

Ingredients

- 1 pound broccoli
- 1 tablespoon chickpea flour
- For marinade
- 1 tablespoon yogurt
- ¼ teaspoon turmeric powder
- ½ teaspoon chili powder
- ½ teaspoon Chat Masala
- 1 pinch salt

Directions

1. Cut broccoli into small florets. Dip florets in the large bowl of water and 2 tablespoons salt for 20-30 minutes to remove different insects.
2. Remove from the salty water, drain well and remove extra water using paper towels.
3. In the bowl mix all ingredients for the marinade: yogurt, turmeric powder, chili powder, Chat Masala.
4. Toss the broccoli florets in the marinade and set aside in the refrigerator for 15-20 minutes.
5. Preheat the Air Fryer to 370-390°F
6. Place marinated broccoli florets into the Fryer basket and cook for 10 minutes.
7. Shake once during cooking. Prepare until become golden and crispy.
8. Serve warm and enjoy.

Turnip Fries

Prep time: 5 minutes, cook time: 45 minutes, serves: 1

Ingredients

- Small Turnip (Rutabaga)
- Spices of your choice (for example Cajun spice and garlic powder)
- 1 Tablespoon olive oil

Directions

1. Wash turnip and dry it with a paper towel.
2. Cut turnip the same thickness as French fries.
3. Put slices in a bowl, drizzle with oil and sprinkle with your favorite spices.
4. Cook in your air fryer for nearly 40-45 minutes until golden and crispy.

Fried Carrots with Cumin

Prep time: 5 minutes, cook time: 20 minutes, serves: 4

Ingredients

- 1 pound carrots, peeled
- 1 tablespoon olive oil
- 1 teaspoon cumin seeds
- 1 handful of fresh coriander, crushed
- A pinch of salt

Directions

1. Wash carrots.
2. Drizzle carrots with olive oil. Sprinkle with cumin seeds and stir to combine.
3. Cook the carrots in the air fryer for approximately 20 minutes at 360 F, until lightly browned and tender.
4. Scatter with crushed coriander.

Crispy Zucchini Drumsticks

Prep time: 10-12 minutes, cook time: 22 minutes, serves: 5

Ingredients

- 3 medium-sized zucchini, cut into thick one size sticks
- ½ cup breadcrumbs (you may also take breadcrumbs with Italian herbs)
- 2 egg whites
- 2 tablespoon Parmesan cheese, grated
- Ground black pepper
- Salt (or garlic salt), to taste

Directions

1. Combine breadcrumbs and grated Parmesan cheese in a medium bowl.
2. Season zucchini drumsticks with salt and pepper, dip them into egg whites and evenly coat with breadcrumbs mixture.
3. Preheat your Air Fryer device to 380°F.
4. Put covered zucchini sticks into the fryer and cook for 15 minutes.

Mushrooms Stuffed with Garlic

Prep time: 10 minutes, cook time: 10 minutes, serves: 4

Ingredients

- 16 small pieces of mushrooms

Ingredients for Stuffing

- 1 ½ slices of white bread
- 1 tablespoon finely chopped flat-leafed parsley
- 1 crushed garlic clove
- 1 ½ tablespoon olive oil
- Ground black pepper to taste

Directions

1. Mix all ingredients in a food processor and stir with olive oil.
2. Mushrooms cut and separate from stalks and the caps fill with the breadcrumbs and other ingredients.
3. Cook for 7-8 minutes on 390°F.
4. Season with black pepper to taste

Stuffed Mushroom Caps

Prep time: 10 minutes, cook time: 5 minutes, serves: 3

Ingredients

- 10 mushrooms
- 4 bacon slices, cut
- ¼ middle onion, diced
- ½ cup cheese, grated
- Ground black pepper and salt to taste

Directions

1. Wash mushrooms, drain well and remove stems.
2. In the middle bowl combine bacon, cut into ½ inch pieces, diced onion and grated cheese.
3. Season mushroom caps with salt and pepper.
4. Put bacon mixture to the seasoned mushroom caps.
5. Preheat the Air Fryer to 380°F
6. Place mushrooms into the Fryer and cook for 5 minutes until cheese melted.
7. Serve and enjoy.

Delicious Breaded Mushrooms

Prep time: 10 minutes, cook time: 7-10 minutes, serves: 3

Ingredients

- 10 oz button mushrooms
- ¼ cup flour
- 1 egg
- ½ cup breadcrumbs
- 3 oz cheese, finely grated
- Salt and pepper for seasoning

Directions

1. In the middle bowl mix breadcrumbs with cheese, season with salt and pepper to taste and set aside.
2. In another middle bowl beat an egg and also set aside.
3. Wash and dry mushrooms with the paper towels.
4. Preheat the Air Fryer to 340-360°F
5. Roll mushrooms in the flour, dip them into the beaten egg and dip in the breadcrumbs and cheese mixture.
6. Place to the Fryer and cook for 7-10 minutes. Shake once while cooking.
7. Serve warm with any sauce you like.

Sautéed Spinach with Bacon, Onion and Garlic

Prep time: 10 minutes, cook time: 15 minutes, serves: 3

Ingredients

- 5 oz spinach or other greens
- 1 small onion cut thinly
- 1 clove garlic minced
- 1 tablespoon spoon olive oil

Directions

1. Peel and cut onion thinly.
2. Preheat air fryer to 350°F.
3. Add onion, garlic and bacon into air fryer and cook for 2-3 minutes.
4. Add the spinach or other greens and cook additionally for 5 minutes or until sautéed but not too much.

Warm Brussels Sprout Salad with Bacon

Prep time: 5 minutes, cook time: 15 minutes, serves: 3

Ingredients

- 1 strip bacon, diced
- 3/4 pound Brussels sprouts
- 1/4 cup water
- 1 tablespoon freshly squeezed lemon juice
- 1/2 tablespoon extra virgin olive oil
- Salt and freshly ground pepper to taste

Directions

1. Preheat air fryer to 340-360°F.
2. Put diced bacon into the air fryer and cook for 7 minutes.
3. Cut off the bottom of each Brussels sprout, pull off outer leaves and slice the core into quarters.
4. Add Brussels sprout leaves and quarters into the air fryer and drizzle with water.
5. Cook for nearly 7 minutes.
6. Put the contents of the air fryer to the serving bowl. Sprinkle the salad with fresh lemon juice and olive oil and season to taste with salt and pepper.

Chicken, Turkey & Duck Recipes

Classic Chicken Spring Rolls

Prep time: 10 minutes, cook time: 20 minutes, serves: 4

Ingredients for Rolls

- 1 beaten egg
- 8 spring rolls wrappers
- 1 teaspoon cornstarch
- ¼ teaspoon vegetable oil

Ingredients for Filling

- 4 oz. cooked and shredded chicken breast
- 1 sliced thin carrot, medium size
- 1 sliced thin celery stalk
- 1 teaspoon sugar
- ½ cup sliced thin mushrooms
- ½ teaspoon finely chopped ginger
- 1 teaspoon chicken stock powder

Directions

1. First, you need to make the filling. Chicken put into a bowl and mix with the carrot, celery, and mushrooms. After that, put ginger, chicken stock powder and sugar and stir.
2. Egg put with cornstarch and mix until it's made paste
3. Now, put filling on roll wrapper, roll it and close with egg.
4. Put rolls brushed with oil into Air fryer on 390°F and cook for 3-4 minutes. Serve with soy or chili sauce.

Chicken Marinated in Mustard

Prep time: 30 minutes, cook time: 20 minutes, serves: 2

Ingredients

- 4 chicken drumsticks
- 2 tablespoons brown sugar
- 1 teaspoon chili powder
- 2 garlic cloves, crushed
- 2 tablespoons mustard
- 1 tablespoon olive oil
- Bundle of rosemary
- Ground pepper and salt to taste

Directions

1. In the large bowl combine crushed garlic, chili powder, olive oil, brown sugar, and mustard.
2. Add salt and ground pepper to taste.
3. Completely dip chicken drumsticks to the marinade and leave for at least for 20 minutes.
4. Preheat the Air Fryer to 360-380°F
5. Place marinated drumsticks to the Fryer and cook for 10 minutes.
6. Then reduce temperature to 280-300°F and cook for another 10 minutes with lower temperature.
7. In 2-3 minutes before finishing add rosemary springs on the top of the drumsticks.
8. Serve warm with mashed potatoes or cooked rice.

Chicken Patties

Prep time: 20 minutes, cook time: 15 minutes, serves: 4

Ingredients

- 1 pound chicken breasts
- 2 medium potatoes, peeled
- 1 small carrot, sliced
- 1 medium onion, sliced
- 1 cup all-purpose flour
- 3 tablespoon vinegar
- 1 teaspoon garlic powder
- ½ teaspoon chili powder
- Salt and black pepper to taste

Directions

1. Cut chicken tenders into ¼ inch pieces. Season with salt, pepper and garlic powder, sprinkle with vinegar and set aside for 30 minutes.
2. Mix all ingredients in a large bowl. Add marinated chicken. Stir to combine.
3. Roll chicken patties with hands and cook in the air fryer for 8-15 minutes at 360 F, until brown and crispy.

Fried Chicken Thighs & Legs

Prep time: 10 minutes, cook time: 20 minutes, serves: 4-6

Ingredients

- 3 chicken legs, bone-in, with skin
- 3 chicken thighs, bone-in, with skin
- 2 cups all-purpose flour
- 1 cup buttermilk
- 1 teaspoon salt
- 1 teaspoon ground black pepper
- 1 teaspoon garlic powder
- 1 teaspoon onion powder
- 1 teaspoon ground cumin
- 2 tablespoons extra virgin olive oil

Directions

1. Wash and dry chicken and transfer to a large bowl. Pour in buttermilk and set aside to a fridge for 2 hours.
2. In another mixing bowl combine flour and all seasonings. Mix well. Dip chicken into the flour mixture, then into the buttermilk and again into the flour.
3. Preheat the air fryer to 360 F and place chicken legs and thighs to the fryer basket. Sprinkle with olive oil and cook for about 20 minutes, turning couple times during cooking, until ready and crispy.
4. Serve with fresh vegetables.

Dijon Lime Chicken

Prep time: 10 minutes, cook time: 10 minutes, serves: 6

Ingredients

- 8 chicken drumsticks
- 1 lime, juiced
- 1 lime zest
- 1 teaspoon salt
- 1 tablespoon light mayonnaise
- ½ teaspoon black pepper
- 2 garlic cloves, minced
- 3 tablespoons Dijon mustard
- 1 teaspoon dried parsley
- 1 tablespoon olive oil

Directions

1. Preheat the air fryer to 370 F. Get rid of the skin of the chicken. Season the chicken with salt and black pepper.
2. In a large bowl mix Dijon mustard with lime juice. Stir in lime zest, minced garlic and parsley. Mix to combine.
3. Cover the chicken with the lime mixture. Set aside for 10-20 minutes.
4. Sprinkle the air fryer with olive oil and add chicken drumsticks. Cook for 5 minutes on each side until cooker and crispy.
5. Serve with mayonnaise.

Breaded Chicken Tender

Prep time: 10 minutes, cook time: 15 minutes, serves: 3

Ingredients

- ¾ pound chicken tenders
- For the breading:
- 2 beaten eggs
- ½ teaspoon salt
- ½ breadcrumbs
- ½ cup flour
- 2 tablespoons olive oil
- 1 teaspoon black pepper

Directions

1. Put the Air fryer to 330°F and prepare the food. You should prepare three bowls - first will be for breadcrumbs, the second one for eggs and the third for flour. In breadcrumbs put olive oil and mix well, so breadcrumb is soaked.
2. The perfect order is rolling chicken in flour, then in eggs and finally into breadcrumbs. Do that with pressure, so make sure that the chicken is coated in breadcrumbs. You can also remove extra breadcrumbs with shaking.
3. Cook in the fryer for 10 minutes on 330°F, then turn up the temperature to 390°F and cook another 5 minutes. The chicken should have golden brown.

Spicy Rolled Meat Servings

Prep time: 10 minutes, cook time: 35 minutes, serves: 4

Ingredients

- 1 pound turkey breast
- 1 garlic clove, minced
- ½ teaspoon chili powder
- 1 teaspoon cinnamon
- 1 ½ teaspoon ground cumin
- 2 tablespoons olive oil
- 1 medium-sized onion, chopped
- 3 tablespoons parsley, chopped

Directions

1. Cut the meat horizontally along the full length about a 1/ 3 of the way from the top stopping 1 inch from the edge. Fold this part open and slit it again from this side and open it.
2. Mix the garlic in a bowl with the chili powder, cinnamon, cumin, pepper and 1 teaspoon salt. Add the olive oil. Spoon 1 tablespoon of this mixture in another small bowl. Mix the onion and parsley in the mixture in the big bowl.
3. Preheat the air fryer to 350 F. Coat the meat with the onion mixture. Roll the meat firmly, start at the short side. Tie the string around the meat at 3 cm intervals. Rub the outside of the rolled meat with the herb mixture.
4. Cook in the air fryer for 30-35 minutes, then serve and enjoy!

Amazing Chicken Breasts with Cream Sauce

Prep time: 5-7 minutes, cook time: 15-18 minutes, serves: 3

Ingredients

- 2 chicken breasts, skinless and boneless
- ½ cup cream
- ½ tablespoon olive oil
- A pinch salt and ground pepper

Directions

1. In a large bowl combine cream, olive oil, season with salt and ground pepper.
2. Preheat the Air Fryer to 350°F.
3. Put the chicken breasts into the bowl. Make sure that all sides are in the mixture.
4. Replace meat in the fryer and cook for 15 minutes or until golden and ready.
5. Serve chicken breasts with fried or fresh vegetables.

Crispy Duck Legs

Prep time: 10 minutes, cook time: 25 minutes, serves: 2

Ingredients

- 2 duck legs
- 1 tablespoon dried thyme
- 1 teaspoon five spice powder
- ½ tablespoon black pepper and salt

Directions

1. Take the duck legs and cover them with the herbs and spices.
2. Preheat the air fryer to 330 F and cook duck legs cook for about 20 minutes. Increase the temperature to 390 F and cook for an extra 5 minutes until crispy.
3. Serve and enjoy.

Mouthwatering Chicken Bites

Prep time: 10 minutes, cook time: 15 minutes, serves: 4

Ingredients

- 1 pound chicken breasts, skinless and boneless
- ¼ cup blue cheese salad dressing
- ¼ cup blue cheese, crumbled
- ½ cup sour cream
- 1 cup breadcrumbs
- 1 tablespoon olive oil
- ½ teaspoon salt
- ¼ teaspoon black pepper

Directions

1. In the large mixing bowl combine salad dressing, sour cream, blue cheese. Stir to combine and set aside.
2. In another bowl combine breadcrumbs, olive oil, salt and pepper. Cut chicken breast to 1-2-inch pieces and place to breadcrumbs mixture. Toss to coat.
3. Preheat the air fryer to 380 F and transfer chicken bites to a frying basket. Cook for 12-15 minutes, until ready and crispy.
4. Serve with sauce and enjoy.

137

KFC Style Crispy Chicken Wings

Prep time: 30 minutes, cook time: 30 minutes, serves: 2

Ingredients

- Chicken wings bone in skin on (6-8)
- Enough low-fat Greek yoghurt to marinade chicken wings
- ½ teaspoon cayenne pepper
- ½ teaspoon white pepper
- ½ teaspoon garlic granules
- ½ teaspoon paprika
- Salt to taste
- ½ teaspoon turmeric
- 1 oz flour
- 1 oz maize flour (corn flour will also work)

Directions

1. Mix all spices with Greek yoghurt and marinade chicken wings at least for 30 minutes but up to 1 day.
2. Add extra spices you like to a mix of flour and maize flour in a large bowl.
3. Dip marinated wings into a flour mix and shake off.
4. Preheat air fryer to 350°F and sprinkle lightly with oil.
5. Cook for 30-35 minutes until golden.

Classic Crispy Chicken Wings

Prep time: 5 minutes, cook time: 35 minutes, serves: 2

Ingredients

- 1 pound chicken wings
- 2 tablespoon Provencal herbs
- 1 teaspoon black ground pepper
- Salt to taste

Directions

1. In the large mixing bowl add chicken wings and coat them evenly with salt, ground pepper, and Provencal herbs. Mix with hands.
2. Preheat the Air Fryer to 370-390°F
3. Spray the cooking basket with a nonstick coating.
4. Place coated wings into the Air Fryer basket and cook for 15-20 minutes. Shake couple times during cooking.
5. Maybe it will need to repeat the operation until all wings become golden.
6. Serve with your favorite dipping sauce (I prefer BBQ but Buffalo, Ranch or Blue Cheese is also OK).
7. Enjoy!

Chicken Drumsticks with Garlic, Lemon and Spices

Prep time: 5 minutes, cook time: 25 minutes, serves: 2

Ingredients

- 1 pound 2 oz skinless chicken drumsticks
- 2 tablespoons fresh coriander leaves
- 1 tablespoon fresh garlic finely chopped
- 3 tablespoons lemon juice
- 1 tablespoon vegetable oil
- Salt to taste

Directions

1. Clean up the chicken drumsticks, drain and put them in the air fryer. Sprinkle with olive oil and cook for about 15-20 minutes or until ready.
2. Add coriander leaves and garlic, stir thoroughly with wooden spoon. Then pour with fresh squeezed lemon juice and cook for another 5 minutes.

Crispy Fried Wings

Prep time: 15 minutes, cook time: 15 minutes, serves: 5

Ingredients

- 3 pounds chicken wings
- 2 tablespoons soy sauce
- 2 tablespoons olive oil
- 6 cloves finely chopped garlic
- 1 finely chopped habanera pepper, without seeds and ribs
- 1 teaspoon cinnamon
- 1 teaspoon white pepper
- 1 tablespoon allspice
- 1 teaspoon cayenne pepper
- 1 teaspoon salt
- 1 tablespoon finely chopped fresh thyme
- 2 tablespoons brown sugar
- 4 finely chopped scallions
- 1 tablespoons grated fresh ginger
- 5 tablespoons lime juice
- ½ cup red wine vinegar

Directions

1. All ingredients mix in a large mixing bowl. Try to cover all chicken and marinade it. It should be in the refrigerator for at least 2 hours, perfectly a whole night.
2. After you removed the wings from all liquid and fat, dry them with a paper towel.
3. Cook wings in an air fryer on 390°F for 16-18 minutes
4. Shake couple of times during cooking.

Spicy Buffalo Chicken Wings

Prep time: 5 minutes, cook time: 15 minutes, serves: 4-5

Ingredients

- 2 pounds chicken wings, excess skin trimmed
- 3 tablespoons butter, melted
- ¼ cup hot sauce (I prefer Tabasco)
- Salt and black pepper to taste

Directions

1. First, you need to prepare the chicken wings. Cut wing tips and excess skin. Then, divide wings in halves and place both parts in a bowl or Ziploc bad.
2. In the bowl combine the melted butter and the hot sauce and mix well.
3. Pour this mixture over the chicken wings and let them marinate for at least 2 hours.
4. Preheat the air fryer to 390 F.
5. Cook the wings for 13-15 minutes, shaking half way through cooking. The wings should be cooked with brown, crispy skin.
6. Serve the wings with any dipping sauce you prefer. Better tastes with blue cheese dip.

Chicken Kebabs

Prep time: 10 minutes, cook time: 15 minutes, serves: 2-3

Ingredients

- 1 pound chicken breasts, diced
- 5 tablespoons honey
- ½ cup soy sauce
- 6 large mushrooms, cut in halves
- 3 medium-sized bell peppers, cut
- 1 small zucchini, cut into rings
- 2 medium tomatoes, cut into rings
- Salt and pepper, to taste
- ¼ cup sesame seeds
- 1 tablespoon olive oil

Directions

1. Cut chicken breasts into cubes and transfer to a large bowl. Add some salt and pepper. Add 1 tablespoon of olive oil and stir to combine. Add honey and soy sauce, and sprinkle with some sesame seeds. Set aside for 15-30 minutes.
2. Cut mushrooms, tomatoes, bell peppers, and zucchini.
3. Take wooden skewers and start putting chicken and vegetables, mixing each other.
4. Preheat the air fryer to 340 F and place chicken kebabs into the fryer basket.
5. Cook for about 15 minutes, turning once during cooking, until crispy and brown.
6. Serve and enjoy.

Stew Turkey with Pumpkin and Nutmeg

Prep time: 10 minutes, cook time: 25 minutes, serves: 4

Ingredients

- 1 pound boneless and skinless turkey breast, cut into cubes
- 12 1/3 oz pumpkin cut into cubes
- 4 tablespoons maple syrup
- 1 sliced onion
- 1 bay leaf
- 1 sprig fresh thyme chopped
- 1 teaspoon nutmeg
- 6 tablespoons cherry jelly or cranberry sauce
- 10 fl oz low-fat chicken stock
- 2 tablespoons oil
- Salt and pepper, to taste

Directions

1. Preheat air fryer to 330-350°F and add oil.
2. Cut turkey into 1-inch cubes, slice onion, season and add to air fryer. Cook for 5 minutes until golden.
3. Add the maple syrup and set aside – let caramelize.
4. Cut pumpkin into 1-inch cubes. Add to the air fryer with nutmeg and cook together for 2-3 minutes.
5. Add chicken stock and herbs. Cook for 15 minutes.
6. Mix the sauce with cherry jelly and cook for another 2 minutes.

Sausage Stuffed in Chicken Fillet

Prep time: 5 minutes, cook time: 15 minutes, serves: 4

Ingredients

- 4 sausages you prefer
- 4 chicken fillets (thigh or breast)
- 8 bamboo skewers or toothpicks

Directions

1. Push and roll chicken meat with a rolling pin.
2. Remove sausage casing.
3. Place sausage meat into the chicken filet.
4. Fold chicken meat into halves and seal by 2 toothpicks into each piece.
5. Preheat the Air Fryer to 390 F, place meat into the frying basket and cook for 15 minutes.
6. Serve with any dipping sauce you like.

Buttermilk Airfried Chicken

Prep time: 10 minutes, cook time: 15 minutes, serves: 8

Ingredients

- 5 chicken breast halves, boneless and skinless
- 1 large egg, beaten
- 1 cup butter milk
- 1 teaspoon garlic powder
- 1 cup plain flour
- 1 cup Italian seasoned breadcrumbs
- ½ cup Parmesan cheese, shredded
- A pinch of cayenne pepper
- 1 teaspoon salt
- 1 teaspoon ground black pepper
- 1 tablespoon olive oil

Directions

1. In the large mixing bowl combine 1 egg, buttermilk, garlic powder, and cayenne pepper. Set aside.
2. Cut chicken breasts into strips and place them in a large Ziploc bag. Pour in the buttermilk mixture and close well. Place Ziploc bag in the refrigerator for 2-3 hours.
3. In another shallow dish combine plain flour, breadcrumbs, grated parmesan cheese, salt and pepper.
4. Preheat the air fryer to 370 F and sprinkle with 1 tablespoon of olive oil.
5. Remove chicken strips from the Ziploc bag and roll in the flour mixture. Make sure that all sides are covered with the mixture.
6. Place the chicken in the air fryer and cook for about 15 minutes, turning once to prevent burning. Cook until crispy and brown.
7. When ready, serve and enjoy.

Old Bay Crispy Chicken Wings

Prep time: 10 minutes, cook time: 40 minutes, serves: 4-5

Ingredients

- 3 pounds bone-in chicken wings
- ¾ cup all-purpose flour
- 1 tablespoon Old Bay Seasoning
- 4 tablespoon butter
- Couple fresh lemons

Directions

1. In the large bowl combine all-purpose flour and Old Bay seasoning. Add chicken wings and toss to combine. Make sure all wings are completely covered with flour mixture.
2. Preheat the air fryer to 375 F. Shake off excess flour from wings and transfer them into air fryer. Work in batches and do not overcrowd the basket.
3. Cook for about 30-40 minutes until wings are ready and skin crispy. Shake often.
4. Meanwhile, melt butter in a sauté pan over low heat. Squeeze lemon juice from one or two lemons to a melted butter and stir to combine.
5. Serve hot wings and pour butter-lemony sauce on top.

Chicken Tenders Baked with Honey

Prep time: 30 minutes, cook time: 6-8 minutes, serves: 4

Ingredients

- 1 pound chicken tenders
- ¼ cup water
- ½ teaspoon red pepper flakes
- 3 tablespoon tamari (aged soy sauce)
- 2 tablespoon honey
- 2 gloves of garlic, minced
- 1 tablespoon peeled and grated ginger
- ¾ cup thinly sliced green onions. Use white part for the marinade. Keep green part for sprinkling on top when done.

Directions

1. Mix water, white parts of onion, soy sauce, honey, garlic and ginger.
2. Cut chicken tenders into stripe pieces and toss into marinade at least for 30 minutes or more.
3. Pour entire mixture into air fryer and cook for about 6-8 minutes. (Sometimes you will need more or less time depending on slices size).
4. Sprinkle with green parts of onion as decoration.

Balsamic Chicken with Vegetables

Prep time: 8 minutes, cook time: 20 minutes, serves: 4

Ingredients

- 8 chicken thighs
- 5 oz mushrooms, sliced
- 1 small onion, diced
- 8 asparagus spears
- 1 small carrot, diced
- 2 garlic cloves, minced
- ¼ cup balsamic vinegar
- 1 teaspoon sugar
- 1 teaspoon fresh rosemary
- 1 teaspoon dried oregano
- 1 teaspoon dried sage
- 1 tablespoon olive oil
- Salt and pepper to taste

Directions

1. Sprinkle baking tray with olive oil.
2. Rub chicken thighs with salt and pepper.
3. Mix all vegetables in a large bowl. Add herbs, sugar, vinegar, mushrooms. Stir to combine.
4. Replace vegetable mixture to the baking tray and also add chicken.
5. Cook in the preheated air fryer for 20 minutes at 380 F.
6. Serve.

BBQ Chicken

Prep time: 15 minutes, cook time: 15 minutes, serves: 3

Ingredients

- 12 oz. (or ¾ pound) boneless chicken tenders without skin
- ½ cup pineapple juice
- ½ cup soy sauce – it would be perfect if you find those with low sodium
- 4 chopped garlic
- ¼ cup sesame oil
- 1 tablespoon grated, fresh ginger
- 4 chopped scallions
- 1 pinch black pepper
- 2 teaspoons toasted sesame seeds

Directions

1. All ingredients mix in a large bowl and add in that chicken. Make sure that chicken is skewered before that, use wooden chops and remove all fat and skin. It's good to put this in refrigerate for at least 2 hours. The perfect time is 24 hours.
2. Air fryer put on 390°F. Before you put the chicken in it, dry it with a paper towel and remove all marinade from it. Don't worry; all important parts are already in chicken. Cook for 5-7 minutes.
3. Enjoy!

Delicious Turkey Breast with Maple Mustard Glaze

Prep time: 5 minutes, cook time: 45 minutes, serves: 6

Ingredients

- 5-pound whole turkey breast, skinless
- ¼ cup maple syrup
- 2 tablespoon mustard
- 1 tablespoon butter
- 2 teaspoons olive oil
- 1 teaspoon dried thyme
- 1 teaspoon dried sage
- 1 teaspoon smoked paprika
- Salt and ground black pepper to taste

Directions

1. Brush the turkey breast with the olive oil.
2. In the mixing bowl combine thyme, sage, paprika, salt and pepper. Rub this mixture outside of the turkey breast.
3. Preheat the air fryer to 350 F.
4. Place the seasoned turkey meat to the air fryer basket and cook for 25 minutes. Turn the turkey breast once in the middle of cooking. You should cook it for 12 minutes on each side.
5. Meanwhile, prepare the glaze. In a saucepan, combine the maple syrup, mustard and butter. When the turkey breast is ready, open the air fryer and brush the glaze all over the meat. Cook for another 5 minutes, until nicely brown and crispy.
6. Let the turkey rest for couple minutes, and then slice it and serve.

Spicy Chicken with Rosemary

Prep time: 15 minutes, cook time: 30 minutes, serves: 4

Ingredients

- 1 whole chicken (4-5 pounds)
- 2 cups potatoes, diced
- ½ large onion, diced
- 3 garlic cloves, minced
- 1 ½ teaspoon black pepper
- 1 ½ teaspoon dried thyme
- 1 ½ teaspoon dried rosemary
- 1 ½ teaspoon dried paprika
- 2 teaspoon olive oil
- 1 ½ teaspoon salt
- Fresh rosemary and sliced lemon for decoration

Directions

1. Clean the chicken inside. Do not cut.
2. Marinate the chicken with 1 teaspoon salt and 1 teaspoon black pepper. Set aside for 20-30 minutes.
3. In the large bowl mix diced potato and diced onion with ½ teaspoon salt and pepper, 1 teaspoon paprika, thyme, and rosemary.
4. In another small bowl mix olive oil, ½ teaspoon dried, ½ dried thyme, minced garlic.
5. Preheat the Air Fryer to 400°F
6. Stuff vegetable mixture into the chicken, and cover it with garlic sauce.
7. Wrap stuffed chicken with foil and cook in the Air Fryer for 30 minutes until chicken will become golden and ready.
8. Replace the chicken to the serving plate take potatoes and onion out of the chicken.
9. Decorate with lemon and fresh rosemary.

Chicken with Butternut Squash

Prep time: 25 minutes, cook time: 20 minutes, serves: 2

Ingredients

- 1 pound chicken breast
- 2 tablespoons thinly sliced fresh sage leaves
- 1 teaspoon Worcestershire sauce
- ½ teaspoon salt
- 1 ½ cups butternut squash, peeled and cut into 1/2 inch cubes
- 1 tablespoon vegetable oil
- ½ cup sliced onion
- Freshly ground pepper

Directions

1. Mix Worcestershire sauce, salt and sage in the large bowl.
2. Wash boneless and skinless chicken breast, cut it into 1-inch pieces, toss into sauce and set aside.
3. Peel butternut squash and cut into ½ inch cubes.
4. Place squash in the air fryer, drizzle with oil and cook for 7 minutes.
5. Add onion and cook for another 5 minutes.
6. Add chicken pieces, stir with a wooden spoon to mix the squash and chicken, cook for 5-7 minutes or until cooked
7. Season with freshly ground pepper to taste.

Chicken-filled Sandwich

Prep time: 10 minutes, cook time: 15 minutes, serves: 2

Ingredients

- 2 chicken breasts, boneless and skinless
- 2 large eggs
- ½ cup skimmed milk
- 6 tablespoons soy sauce
- 1 cup all-purpose flour
- 1 teaspoon smoked paprika
- 1 teaspoon salt
- ¼ teaspoon black pepper
- ½ teaspoon garlic powder
- 1 tablespoon olive oil
- 4 Hamburger buns

Directions

1. Cut chicken breast into 2-3 pieces, depending on its size. Transfer to a large bowl and sprinkle with soy sauce. Season with smoked paprika, black pepper, salt, and garlic powder and stir to combine. Set aside for 30-40 minutes.
2. Meanwhile, combine eggs with milk in a mixing bowl. In another bowl place all-purpose flour.
3. Dip marinated chicken into egg mixture and then into flour. Make sure pieces are coated with all ingredients.
4. Preheat the air fryer to 380 F. Sprinkle with olive oil and place chicken pieces into the fryer. Cook for 10-12 minutes, turning once, until ready.
5. Toast Hamburger buns and assemble sandwiches. You may also use ketchup, BBQ sauce or any other for your preference. Enjoy!

Fried Whole Chicken with Potatoes

Prep time 2 minutes, cook time 35-40 minutes, serves: 6

Ingredients

- 1 whole fresh chicken (2-3 pounds)
- 1 pound potatoes
- 2 tablespoon Italian seasoning
- 1 tablespoon olive oil
- Salt and black pepper to taste

Directions

1. Cover the whole chicken with Italian seasoning inside and outside. Also season with salt and pepper to taste.
2. Preheat the Air Fryer to 390 F. Put chicken into Fryer and cook for 15-20 minutes depending on size of the chicken.
3. Meanwhile, wash potatoes and dry with kitchen towels. Put potatoes in the large mixing bowl and drizzle with the olive oil. Season with salt and pepper slightly and add to the Air Fryer. Place potatoes around the chicken. Cook additionally for 15-20 minutes, until chicken and potatoes become ready.

Tip: you can marinate the chicken or fill it with any stuffing if desired.

Crispy Chicken Meatballs

Prep time: 20 minutes, cook time: 14 minutes, serves: 3

Ingredients

- 1 pound chicken breasts, skinless and boneless
- 1 large or 2 medium potatoes, pilled
- 1 medium carrot
- ½ green bell pepper, seeded and sliced
- 1 cup flour
- 2 tablespoons heated oil
- 1 teaspoon garlic paste
- ¼ teaspoon brown sugar
- 1 teaspoon chili powder
- Ground black pepper and salt to taste

Directions

1. Cut chicken breasts into ¼ inch pieces. Cover it with garlic paste, season with salt and ground pepper and set aside for couple hours.
2. In the large bowl mix flour, chili powder, brown sugar, heated oil. Stir to combine.
3. Cut potatoes, carrot and green bell pepper into ¼ inch pieces.
4. Add vegetables and marinated chicken into the flour mixture, mix thoroughly, roll medium-sized meatballs and place them on a baking sheet.
5. Preheat the Air Fryer to 350-370°F
6. Place chicken meatballs in the fryer for 10-12 minutes until they become golden and crispy.
7. Serve with mayonnaise or your favorite dip sauce.

Chicken Fillet with Brie & Ham

Prep time 15 minutes, cook time: 15 minutes, serves: 4

Ingredients

- 2 large chicken fillets
- Freshly ground pepper
- 4 small slices Brie cheese
- 1 tablespoon chives, chopped
- 4 slices cured ham
- 4 tablespoons olive oil

Directions

1. Preheat the air fryer to 360 F. Cut the chicken fillets into four equal pieces and slit them horizontally to ½ inch from the edge. Open the chicken fillets and sprinkle with salt and pepper. Cover each piece with a slice of Brie and some chives.
2. Close the chicken fillets and tightly wrap a slice of ham around them. Thinly coat the stuffed fillets with olive oil and put them in the air fryer. Cook for 15 minutes until brown and ready. Enjoy!

Air-fried Turkey with Sweet Chili Sauce

Prep time: 15 minutes, cook time: 7 minutes, serves: 5-6

Ingredients

- ½ pound leftover turkey breast
- 4 tablespoons breadcrumbs
- 2 tablespoons gluten free oats
- 2 oz cheese, grated
- 1 large eggs
- 1 teaspoon dried thyme
- 1 teaspoon dried parsley
- Salt and black pepper to taste
- For Sauce
- 1 red chili, cored and chopped
- 4 garlic cloves, minced
- 4 tablespoons sugar

Directions

1. First, preheat the air fryer to 370 F.
2. In large mixing bowl combine together gluten free oats, grated cheese, and breadcrumbs. Also add dried herbs to the mixture. Combine well.
3. In another bowl beat the egg.
4. Cut the turkey into stripes, lay out on a working surface and season with salt and pepper from all sides. Then, dip turkey into the egg and then roll on in the breadcrumb mixture.
5. Place coated turkey to the air fryer basket and cook for 7 minutes. Then, turn the meat and cook for another 5 minutes, until done and crispy.
6. Meanwhile, you may cook the sweet chili sauce. In the large bowl place sugar and pour in the same amount of cold water. Bring this mixture to a boil over the high heat. Add chili pepper and minced garlic and reduce the heat. Simmer the sauce for 10 minutes, until it has reduced. Cool the sauce in the refrigerator for 10-15 minutes and serve with crispy turkey.

Easy Blackened Chicken

Prep time: 3 minutes, cook time: 10 minutes, serves: 2

Ingredients

- 2 medium-sized chicken breasts, skinless and boneless
- ½ teaspoon salt
- tablespoons Cajun spice
- 1 tablespoon olive oil

Directions

1. Rub chicken breasts with salt, Cajun spice and sprinkle with olive oil.
2. Preheat the air fryer to 370 F and cook chicken breasts for 7 minutes. Turn to another side and cook for another 3-4 minutes.
3. When ready, slice and serve.

Oil-Free Chicken Fingers

Prep time: 8 minutes, cook time: 18 minutes, serves: 3

Ingredients

- 2 chicken tenders, cut into 1-inch stripes
- 2 large eggs beaten
- ½ cup all-purpose flour
- 1 teaspoon dried dill
- Salt, to taste
- Sauce for serving, to taste

Directions

1. Preheat the air fryer to 370 F.
2. In the large plate combine flour with salt and dried dill and set aside.
3. In another bowl beat eggs. Dip chicken stripes into the egg mixture and then into the flour mixture. Shake well to delete excess coating and place chicken sticks to the air fryer.
4. Cook for 15-18 minutes until golden brown and ready.
5. Serve with sauce and enjoy!

Korean Chicken

Prep time: 10 minutes, cook time: 13 minutes, serves: 3

Ingredients

- 1 pound chicken breasts
- 3 garlic cloves, crushed
- 1 tablespoon grated ginger
- ¼ teaspoon ground black pepper
- ½ cup soy sauce
- ½ cup pineapple juice
- 1 tablespoon olive oil
- 2 tablespoon sesame seeds

Directions

1. Mix all ingredients in the large bowl.
2. Cut chicken breasts and soak in the marinade. Set aside for at least 30-40 minutes.
3. Cook marinated chicken in the air fryer at 380 F for about 10-15 minutes.
4. Sprinkle cooked chicken with sesame seeds and serve.

Chicken with Spaghetti

Prep time: 5 minutes, cook time: 15 minutes, serves:

Ingredients

- 1 pound chicken tenders
- 2 tablespoon sugar
- ¾ cup soy sauce
- ½ cup mirin
- 1 tablespoon grated ginger
- 1 medium carrot, chopped
- 2 small onions, sliced
- 1 pack spaghetti
- Salt and pepper to taste

Directions

1. Cut chicken into bite-size pieces and place in the round baking tray.
2. Add sugar, soy sauce, mirin, grated ginger, carrots, and onions. Mix well.
3. Place the baking tray to the air fryer and cook for about 15 minutes at 320 F.
4. Meanwhile, cook spaghetti in salted water.
5. When ready, mix chicken with spaghetti and serve.

Delicious Turkey Patties

Prep time: 8 minutes, cook time: 10 minutes, serves: 6

Ingredients

- 1 pound ground turkey
- ½ pound fresh mushrooms
- 2 garlic cloves, minced
- 1 small onion, chopped
- Salt and black pepper to taste
- Cooking spray

Directions

1. First, you need to prepare mushrooms. Rinse them well, place into food processor and make a puree. Season with salt and pepper, add minced garlic and chopped onion and pulse for 30 seconds more.
2. Transfer the mushroom mixture to a large plate and add ground turkey. Combine well with spoon or hands.
3. Divide the mixture to six equal pieces and shape patties.
4. Preheat the air fryer to 340 F and place the patties into the frying basket. Cook for 10 minutes until patties become tender.
5. Serve hot with mashed potatoes or steamed rice.

Air Fryer Turkey

Prep time: 8 minutes, cook time: 20 minutes, serves: 4

Ingredients

- 2 pounds turkey breasts, boneless
- 1 tablespoon coconut sugar
- 1/2 teaspoon black pepper
- 1 tablespoon olive oil
- 1 large tomato, sliced
- ¼ pound Cheddar cheese, sliced
- A pinch of salt, to taste

Directions

1. Preheat the air fryer to 380 F.
2. In a large mixing bowl combine coconut sugar, salt, pepper, and olive oil. Cut each turkey breast lengthwise but leave attached at the end. Put sliced tomato and Cheddar cheese between the cut sides of the turkey breasts. Coat with the coconut sugar mixture.
3. Place in the air fryer and cook for 20-25 minutes or until cooked and browned.
4. Serve and enjoy!

Crispy Chicken Fillet with Cheese

Prep time: 10 minutes, cook time: 15 minutes, serves: 4

Ingredients

- 2 pounds chicken tenders
- ½ cup Parmesan cheese
- 1 cup breadcrumbs
- 1 oz butter, melted
- 1 egg
- 1 teaspoon garlic powder
- 1 teaspoon Italian herbs

Directions

1. In the large bowl mix beaten egg, melted butter, garlic powder and, Italian herbs.
2. Marinate chicken tenders into the mixture for at least 30 minutes.
3. I another bowl mix breadcrumbs with Parmesan cheese.
4. Cover chicken meat with breadcrumb mixture and leave for 5 minutes.
5. Preheat the Air Fryer to 350°F
6. Place chicken tenders into the fryer and cook for 5-6 minutes. Then flip to another side and cook for another 3-5 minutes, until chicken becomes golden and ready.
7. Serve immediately with dipping sauce you prefer.

Fried Turkey Breast

Prep time: 5 minutes, cook time: 25 minutes, serves: 6

Ingredients

- 5 pounds turkey breast, skinless and boneless
- 2 teaspoons salt
- 1 teaspoon black pepper
- ½ teaspoon dried cumin
- 2 tablespoons olive oil

Directions

1. Rub the whole turkey breast with all seasoning and olive oil.
2. Preheat the air fryer to 340 F and cook turkey breast for 15 minutes. When time gone, flip the breast to another side and cook for 10-15 minutes more, until ready and crispy.
3. Slice and serve meat with mashed rice or fresh vegetables.

Delicious Chicken Quesadillas

Prep time: 5 minutes, cook time: 10 minutes, serves: 4

Ingredients

- 2 soft taco shells
- 1 pound chicken breasts, boneless
- 1 large green pepper, sliced
- 1 medium-sized onion, sliced
- ½ cup Cheddar cheese, shredded
- ½ cup salsa sauce
- 2 tablespoons olive oil
- Salt and pepper, to taste

Directions

1. Preheat the air fryer to 370 F and sprinkle the basket with 1 tablespoon of olive oil.
2. Place 1 taco shell on the bottom of the fryer.
3. Spread salsa sauce on the taco. Cut chicken breast into stripes and lay on taco shell.
4. Place onions and peppers on the top of the chicken. Sprinkle with salt and pepper. Then, add shredded cheese and cover with second taco shell.
5. Sprinkle with 1 tablespoon of olive oil and put the rack over taco to hold it in place.
6. Cook for 4-6 minutes, until cooked and lightly brown.
7. Cut and serve either hot or cold.

Bacon Wrapped Chicken

Prep time: 10 minutes, cook time: 15 minutes, serves: 2

Ingredients

- 1 pound chicken tender, skinless and boneless
- 4-6 bacon stripes
- 4 tablespoon brown sugar
- ½ teaspoon chili powder

Directions

1. In the large bowl mix brown sugar and chili powder.
2. Cut chicken tenders into 2-inch pieces.
3. Wrap chicken pieces into bacon strips and toss with sugar mixture.
4. Preheat the Air Fryer to 390-400°F
5. Place wrapped chicken into the Fryer and cook for about 10-15 minutes depending on the size of the chicken.
6. Replace the meal from the cooking basket and enjoy crispy bacon and tender, juicy chicken. You may use dipping sauce you prefer.

Asian Style Chicken

Prep time: 10 minutes, cook time: 13 minutes, serves: 3

Ingredients

- 1 pound chicken breasts, skinless and boneless
- 3 garlic cloves, minced
- 1 tablespoon grated ginger
- ¼ teaspoon ground black pepper
- ½ cup soy sauce
- ½ cup pineapple juice
- 1 tablespoon olive oil
- 2 tablespoon sesame seeds

Directions

1. Mix all ingredients in the large bowl.
2. Cut chicken breasts and soak in the marinade. Set aside for at least 30-40 minutes.
3. Cook marinated chicken in the air fryer at 380 F for about 10-15 minutes.
4. Sprinkle cooked chicken with sesame seeds and serve.

Roasted Orange Duck

Prep time: 10 minutes, cook time: 20 minutes, serves: 3-4

Ingredients

- 1 pound duck breast, cut
- 1 teaspoon chili powder
- 1 teaspoon garlic powder
- 1 cup orange juice, freshly squeezed
- Salt and black pepper to taste

Directions

1. Cut duck breast into 2-inch pieces and place to the large mixing bowl. Pour in orange juice; add chili powder, garlic powder and season with salt and pepper. Set aside and let the duck meat marinate for at least 30 minutes.
2. Preheat the air fryer to 380 F.
3. Place the marinated duck breast into the frying basket and cook for about 15-20 minutes, depending of thickness of the meat. The duck should be brown and crispy.
4. Serve with fresh of steamed vegetables and enjoy!

Pork Recipes

Sweet and Sour Delicious Pork

Prep time: 15 minutes, cook time: 20 minutes, serves: 4

Ingredients

- 1 pound 5 oz pork tenderloin, trimmed of fat, cut into strips
- 1 tablespoon corn flour (+ extra for coating)
- 4 fl oz red wine
- 10 fl oz tomato sauce or passata
- 1 tablespoon tomato paste or tomato puree
- 5 fl oz unsweetened apple juice
- 2 tablespoons brown sugar
- 2 sliced onions
- 2 cloves finely chopped garlic (optional)
- 2 tablespoons red wine vinegar
- 2 tablespoons olive oil
- Salt and freshly ground pepper to taste

Directions

1. Mix in a large bowl corn flour with red wine until smooth than add there: tomato sauce, apple juice, vinegar, sugar, tomato paste, season and mix thoroughly. Set bowl aside.
2. Coat chopped meat in corn flour and set aside.
3. Slice onions and put them into air fryer. Pour the olive oil over them. Cook for 5 minutes.
4. Add coated with flour pork and finely chopped garlic (optional). Cook for another 5 minutes.
5. Stir the pork to separate the pieces and add them to the sweet and sour sauce. Cook for 10 minutes or until the pork tender and the sauce thick.
6. Season to taste.

Country Fried Steak

Prep time: 10 minutes, cook time: 12-15 minutes, serves: 2

Ingredients

- 2 pieces 6-ounce sirloin steak pounded thin
- 4 eggs, beaten
- 1 ½ cup all-purpose flour
- 1 ½ cup breadcrumbs
- 1 teaspoon onion powder
- 1 teaspoon garlic powder
- 1 teaspoon salt
- ½ teaspoon pepper

Directions

1. Combine the breadcrumbs, onion, and garlic powder, salt and pepper.
2. In other bowls place flour and beat eggs.
3. Dip the steak in this order: flour, eggs, and seasoned breadcrumbs.
4. Cook breaded steak for 6-7 minute at 380 F, turn over once and cook for another 5-7 minutes until becomes golden and crispy.

Easy Cooking Pork Chop

Ingredients

- 2 middle pieces pork chop
- 1 tablespoon plain flour
- 1 egg, beaten
- 2 tablespoon olive oil
- 3 tablespoon breadcrumbs
- Salt and ground pepper for seasoning

Directions

1. Season pork chop with salt and ground pepper from both sides.
2. In three different bowls place plain flour, beaten egg, and breadcrumbs.
3. Coat each pork chop from both sides first with flour then with egg and with breadcrumbs.
4. Preheat the Air Fryer to 380°F
5. Place coated pork chops into the Fryer and cook for 10 minutes from one side and 5 minutes from another side.
6. Serve with cooked rice and mashed potatoes.

Char Siu

Prep time: 5 minutes, cook time: 15 minutes, serves: 2

Ingredients

- 1 pound pork
- 3 tablespoon hoisin sauce
- 3 tablespoon sugar
- 3 tablespoon soy sauce
- 2 tablespoon corn syrup
- 2 tablespoon mirin
- 2 tablespoon olive oil
- Salt and pepper to taste

Directions

1. Cut pork into 2-inch stripes.
2. Mix all ingredients besides oil together in a large bowl and then put the meat into marinade. Set aside at least for 40 minutes.
3. Discard marinade and sprinkle pork with olive oil.
4. Cook in the air fryer preheated to 380 F for 15 minutes.
5. Serve.

Pork Satay with Peanut Sauce

Prep time: 20 minutes, cook time: 10 minutes, serves: 3-4

Ingredients

- 1 pound pork chops, cut into 1-inch cubes
- 2 garlic, minced
- 1 tablespoon fresh ginger, grated
- 2 teaspoons chili paste
- 2-3 tablespoons sweet soy sauce
- 2 tablespoons vegetable oil
- 1 shallot, finely chopped
- 1 teaspoon ground coriander
- ½ cup coconut milk
- 4 oz unsalted butter

Directions

1. Mix half of the garlic in a dish with the ginger, 1 teaspoon hot pepper sauce, 1 tablespoon soy sauce, and 1 tablespoon oil. Add the the meat to the mixture and leave to marinate for 15 minutes.
2. Preheat the air fryer to 380 F. Put the marinated meat in the air fryer basket cook for 12 minutes until brown and done. Turn once while cooking.
3. Meanwhile, make the peanut sauce. Heat 1 tablespoon of the oil in a saucepan and gently sauté the shallot with garlic. Add the coriander and cook for 1-2 minutes more. Mix the coconut milk and the peanuts with 1 teaspoon hot pepper sauce and 1 tablespoon soy sauce with the shallot mixture and gently boil for 5 minutes, stirring constantly.
4. Serve the meat with sauce and enjoy!

Zero Oil Pork Chops

Prep time: 5 minutes, cook time: 15 minutes, serves: 2

Ingredients

- 2 pieces pork chops
- 1 tablespoon of plain flour
- 1 large egg
- 2 tablespoon breadcrumbs
- Salt and black pepper to taste

Directions

1. First, you need to preheat the air fryer to 360 F.
2. Then, season pork chops with salt and black pepper and set aside.
3. Beat the egg in the plate. In another plate place the flour and in the third plate - breadcrumbs.
4. Cover each pork chop with the flour on both sides, then, dip in the egg, then, cover with breadcrumbs. Make sure that meat covered from all sides.
5. Place pork chops in the air fryer and cook for 15 minutes, until they are tender and crispy. Turn once while cooking, to cook the meat from both sides.
6. Serve with fresh vegetables or mashed potatoes.

Delicious Pork Tenderloin

Prep time: 15 minutes, cook time: 15 minutes, serves: 2

Ingredients

- 1 pound pork tenderloin
- 1 medium red or yellow pepper, sliced
- 1 large red onion, sliced
- 2 tablespoon Provencal herbs
- 1 tablespoon Olive oil
- ½ tablespoon mustard
- Ground black pepper
- Salt, to taste

Directions

1. In the large bowl mix sliced pepper and onion, Provencal herbs, salt and ground pepper to taste. Also, add olive oil to this mixture.
2. Cut the pork tenderloin into 4-6 large pieces, scrub with salt, ground pepper, and mustard.
3. Preheat your Air Fryer to 370-390° F.
4. Place vegetable mixture to the air fryer.
5. Coat meat pieces with olive oil and place them up to the vegetables.
6. Cook for 15 minutes until meat and vegetables will become roasted.
7. Turn the meat and vegetable in the middle of cooking process.

Drunken Ham with Mustard

Prep time: 10 minutes, cook time: 40 minutes, serves: 4

Ingredients

- 1 joint of ham, approximately 1-2 pounds
- 2 tablespoon honey
- 2 tablespoon French mustard
- 8 oz whiskey
- 1 teaspoon Provencal herbs
- 1 tablespoon salt

Directions

1. In a large casserole dish that fits in your Air Fryer prepare the marinade: combine the whiskey, honey and mustard.
2. Place the ham in the oven dish and turn it in the marinade.
3. Preheat the Air Fryer to 380 F and cook the ham for 15 minutes.
4. Add another shot of whiskey and turn in the marinade again. Cook the ham for 25 minutes until done.
5. Serve with potatoes and fresh vegetables.

Empanadas with Pumpkin and Pork

Prep time: 15 minutes, cook time: 25 minutes, servings: 3

Ingredients

- 1 pound ground pork
- 1 small onion, chopped
- 1 cups pumpkin purée
- 1 red chili pepper, minced
- A pinch of cinnamon
- ½ teaspoon dried thyme
- 2 tablespoons olive oil
- 3 tablespoons water
- Salt and freshly ground black pepper
- 1 package of 10 empanada discs, thawed

Directions

1. First, you need to prepare filling. Preheat your sauté pan over medium-high heat. Add ground pork and chopped onions and sauté for about 5 minutes. The pork should be brown and the onions are soft. Drain the fat from the pan and discard.
2. Then, add the pumpkin purée, water, red chili pepper, cinnamon, thyme to the sauté pan. Season with salt and pepper and combine evenly. Simmer the mixture for 10 minutes. Remove the pan from the heat and set aside to chill.
3. Place the empanada discs on a flat surface and brush the edges with water. Place couple tablespoons of the filling in the center of each disc. Fold the dough over the filling to form a half moon. Brush both sides of the empanadas with olive oil.
4. Preheat the air fryer to 360 F.
5. Place 3 to 5 empanadas into the air fryer basket depending of the size of your empanadas. Do not overload the air fryer. Cook for 14 minutes, turning over after 8 minutes. Serve warm.

Easy Steak Sticks

Prep time: 5 minutes, cook time: 20 minutes, serves: 3

Ingredients

- 1 pound steak
- 2 tablespoon olive oil
- 1 teaspoon dried thyme
- 1 teaspoon dried parsley
- A pinch of chili powder
- Salt and pepper to taste
- Sesame seeds for garnish

Directions

1. Cut the steak into 1-inch strips.
2. In the mixing bowl combine the olive oil and dried herbs. Add chili powder and stir to combine.
3. Preheat the air fryer to 370 F.
4. Lay meat strips to the working surface. Evenly season meat with salt and black pepper. Skewer the steak strips to the skewers. Dip the meat in the oil mixture and place to the air fryer basket. Cook for 15-20 minutes, until brown and crispy.
5. Serve with cooked rice or mashed potatoes. You can also garnish the meat with sesame seeds and freshly chopped herbs of your choice.

Pork Loin with Potatoes and Herbs

Prep time: 10 minutes, cook time: 30 minutes, serves: 4

Ingredients

- 2-pound pork loin
- 2 large potatoes, large dice
- ½ teaspoon garlic powder
- ½ teaspoon red pepper flakes
- 1 teaspoon dried parsley, crushed
- ½ teaspoon black pepper, freshly ground
- A pinch of salt
- Balsamic glaze to taste

Directions

1. Sprinkle the pork loin with garlic powder, red pepper flakes, parsley, salt, and pepper.
2. Preheat the air fryer to 370 F and place the pork loin, then the potatoes next to the pork in the basket of the air fryer and close. Cook for about 20-25 minutes.
3. Remove the pork loin from the air fryer. Let it rest for a few minutes before slicing.
4. Place the roasted potatoes to the serving plate. Slice the pork. Place 4-5 slices over the potatoes and drizzle the balsamic glaze over the pork.

Pork Chops Fried

Prep time: 20 minutes; cook time: 25 minutes, serves: 3

Ingredients

- 3-4 pieces pork chops (cut in 1-inch thick, roughly 10 oz each)
- ¼ cup olive oil, divided
- 1 tablespoon cilantro, chopped
- 1 tablespoon parsley, chopped
- 1 tablespoon rosemary, chopped
- 1 tablespoon Dijon mustard
- 1 tablespoon coriander, ground
- 1-2 teaspoon salt to taste
- 1 teaspoon sugar

Directions

1. In the large mixing bowl combine 1/4 cup olive oil, 1 tablespoon cilantro, parsley, rosemary, Dijon mustard, coriander. Add some salt and black pepper. Dip the meat to the mixture, then transfer to a re-sealable bag and refrigerate for 2-3 hours.
2. Preheat the Air Fryer to 390°F.
3. Remove the pork chops out of the refrigerator and let sit at room temp for 30 minutes prior to cooking.
4. Reheat the Air Fryer to 390°F.
5. Cook 1 to 2 pork chops in the Air Fryer for 10-12 minutes. Please note: thinner cuts will cook faster. Take 2 minutes off the cooking time for thinner cuts. The pork chop will be done when it has reached an internal temperature of 140°F
6. Serve with mashed potatoes or other garnish you prefer.

Chinese Roast Pork

Prep time: 5 minutes, cook time: 25 minutes, serves: 4

Ingredients

- 2 pounds of pork shoulder
- 2 tablespoons sugar
- 1 tablespoon honey
- 1/3 cup of soy sauce
- 1/2 tablespoon salt

Directions

1. Cut the meat in large pieces. Place to a large bowl and add all ingredients to make a marinade. Stir to combine well to coat all the meat pieces.
2. Preheat the air fryer to 350 F. Transfer marinated meat and cook for about 10 minutes, stirring couple times while cooking.
3. Increase the temperature to 400 F and cook for another 3-5 minutes until completely cooked.

Mouth Watering Pork Tenderloin with Bell Pepper

Prep time: 7 minutes, cook time: 15 minutes, serves: 3

Ingredients

- 1 pound pork tenderloin
- 2 medium-sized yellow or red bell peppers, cut into strips
- 1 little onion, sliced
- 2 teaspoons Provencal herbs
- Salt and black pepper to taste
- 1 tablespoon olive oil

Directions

1. In the large mixing bowl combine sliced bell peppers, onions, and Provencal herbs. Season with salt and pepper to taste. Sprinkle with the olive oil and set aside.
2. Cut the pork tenderloin into 1-inch cubes and rub with salt and black pepper.
3. Preheat the air fryer to 370 F.
4. On the bottom of the air fryer basket lay seasoned meat and coat with vegetable mixture. Fry for 15 minutes, turning the meat and veggies once while cooking.
5. Serve with mashed potatoes.

Cheesy Pork Fillets

Prep time: 8 minutes, cook time: 20 minutes, serves: 3

Ingredients

- 3 pork filets
- 2 large eggs, beaten
- 1 cup all-purpose flour
- 3 slices swiss cheese
- Salt and black pepper to taste

Directions

1. Preheat the air fryer to 380 F.
2. Dip pork fillets in egg and top each fillet with cheese slice. Season with salt and pepper and cover each piece with little more egg and then coat in all-purpose flour.
3. Place these "patties" in the air fryer and cook for 20 minutes, turning once during cooking.
4. When ready, serve hot and enjoy!

Beef Recipes

Beef with Broccoli

Prep time: 20 minutes, cook time: 25 minutes, serves: 3

Ingredients

- 2 ½ tablespoons - cornstarch, divided
- ½ cup water
- ½ teaspoon garlic, minced
- 2 8oz New York Steaks
- 1 ½ tablespoons vegetable oil
- 4 cups broccoli florets
- 1 onion, cut into wedges
- 1/3 cup reduced sodium soy sauce
- 2 tablespoons - brown sugar
- 1 teaspoon - ground ginger

Directions

1. Mix in a large bowl: cornstarch, water, minced garlic.
2. Cut beef into 6mm wide strips and coated in the mixture.
3. Put beef into air fryer, pour with oil and cook for 10 minutes. Then remove and set aside.
4. Add broccoli and onion to air fryer, pour with oil and cook for 8 minutes.
5. Combine in a bowl ginger, brown sugar, soy sauce, remaining cornstarch and water.
6. Add beef and sauce mixture to the air fryer and cook for 6-8 minutes.

Healthy Beef Schnitzel

Prep time: 10 minutes, cook time: 12 minutes, serves: 2

Ingredients

- 3 tablespoons olive oil
- 2 oz breadcrumbs
- 2 whisked eggs
- 2 thin beef schnitzels
- 1 lemon to serve

Directions

1. Preheat air fryer to 360°F
2. In the large bowl mix olive oil and breadcrumbs. Keep moving until the mixture become loose and friable.
3. Dip the beef schnitzel into the egg.
4. Then dip the schnitzel into crumb mixture. Make sure it is evenly covered with crumbs.
5. Lay schnitzel to the bottom of fryer basket and cook for nearly 12 minutes. (Time of preparation may vary depending on the thickness of the schnitzel.
6. Serve with lemon and enjoy!

Ground Beef

Ingredients

- 2 tablespoons olive oil
- 1 medium onion, chopped
- 1 pound ground beef
- 1 bunch fresh spinach
- Salt and black pepper, to taste

Directions

1. Grease the baking tray with the olive oil.
2. Preheat the air fryer to 330 F. Add chopped onion to the tray and cook in the fryer for 2-3 minutes, stirring often. Add ground beef, mix well and cook for another 10 minutes, stirring occasionally.
3. Add chopped spinach, season with salt and pepper, stir to combine. Cook for 2-4 minutes until ready.
4. Serve and enjoy!

Crispy Beef Cubes

Prep time: 10 minutes, cook time: 18 minutes, serves: 4

Ingredients

- 1 pound beef loin
- 1 jar (16 oz) cheese pasta sauce
- 6 tablespoons breadcrumbs
- Salt and black pepper, to taste
- 1 tablespoon extra virgin olive oil

Directions

1. Cut beef into 1-inch cubes and transfer to a mixing bowl and coat with pasta sauce.
2. In another bowl combine breadcrumbs, olive oil, salt and pepper. Mix well.
3. Place beef cubes to a breadcrumb mixture and coat from all sides.
4. Preheat the air fryer to 380 F. Cook beef cubes for 12-15 minutes, stirring occasionally, until ready and crispy.
5. Serve hot.

Rolled Up Tender Beef

Prep time: 10 minutes, cook time: 20 minutes, serves: 4

Ingredients

- 2 pound beef steak
- 5-6 slices Cheddar cheese
- ½ cup fresh baby spinach
- 4 tablespoons Pesto
- 2 tablespoons unsalted butter
- 1 teaspoon salt
- ¼ teaspoon black pepper
- 1 tablespoon olive oil

Directions

1. Open beef steak and spread the butter over the meat. Then cover it with pesto.
2. Layer cheese slices, baby spinach and season with salt and pepper. Roll up the meat and secure with toothpicks. Season with salt and pepper again.
3. Preheat the air fryer to 390 F and sprinkle frying basket with olive oil.
4. Place beef roll in the air fryer and cook for 15-20 minutes, turning couple times to roast from all sides.
5. Slice beef roll and serve with mashed potatoes or steamed rice.

Veal Rolls with Sage

Prep time: 15 minutes, cook time: 15 minutes, serves: 4

Ingredients

- 15 oz meat or chicken stock
- 7 oz dry white wine
- 4 veal cutlets
- Freshly ground pepper
- 8 fresh sage leaves
- 4 slices ham
- 2 tablespoons butter

Directions

1. Preheat the air fryer to 380 F.
2. Boil the meat stock and the wine in a wide pan on medium heat until it has reduced to one-third of the original amount.
3. Sprinkle salt and pepper on the cutlets and cover them with the sage leaves. Firmly roll the cutlets and wrap a slice of ham around each cutlet. Thinly brush the entire cutlets with butter and place them in the basket.
4. Slide the basket into the air fryer and cook for 10 minutes. Roast the veal rolls until nicely brown. Lower the temperature to 302 F and cook for another 5 minutes.
5. Mix the remainder of the butter with the reduced stock and season the gravy with salt and pepper. Thinly slice the veal rolls and serve them with the gravy. Serve.

Air Fryer Chipotle Beef

Prep time: 10 minutes, cook time: 30 minutes, serves: 6

Ingredients

- 3 pounds beef eye
- 4 garlic cloves, minced
- 1 tablespoon ground cumin
- 2 teaspoons salt
- 1 small onion
- 3 tablespoons chipotles in adobo sauce
- 1 cup water
- ½ teaspoons ground cloves
- ½ teaspoons black pepper
- 1 tablespoon olive oil
- 1 tablespoon ground oregano

Directions

1. Add garlic cloves, cumin, lime juice, oregano, onion, chipotles, water and cloves in a food processor. Blend until it becomes smooth.
2. Cut the beef into medium size pieces. Season the meat with salt and black pepper. Preheat the air fryer to 400 F. Sprinkle some oil in it. Add the beef and cook for about 5 minutes.
3. Add the mixture from food processor to the air fryer. Stir to coat the beef perfectly and cook for 25 minutes, stirring occasionally. Cook until ready and serve.

Greek Meatballs with Feta

Prep time: 10 minutes, cook time: 10 minutes, serves: 2

Ingredients

- ½ pound ground beef
- 1 slice white bread, crumbled
- ¼ cup feta cheese, crumbled
- 1 tablespoon fresh oregano, chopped
- 1 tablespoon fresh parsley, chopped
- ½ teaspoon ground black pepper
- A pinch of salt

Directions

1. In the large mixing bowl combine ground beef, breadcrumbs, fresh herbs, ground pepper and salt. Mix well to receive smooth paste.
2. Divide the mixture into 8-10 equal pieces.
3. Wet your hands and roll meatballs.
4. Preheat the Air Fryer to 370-390°F
5. Place meatballs into the Fryer and cook for 8-10 minutes, depending on the size of your meatballs.
6. Serve with rice or pasta.

Rib Eye Steak

Prep time: 5 minutes, cook time: 15-20 minutes, serves: 4

Ingredients

- 2 pounds rib eye steak
- 1 tablespoon steak rub
- 1 tablespoon olive oil

Directions

1. Preheat your Air Fryer to 390-400 F.
2. Season the steak on both sides with rub and sprinkle with olive oil.
3. Cook the steak for about 7-8 minutes, rotate the steak and cook for another 6-7 minute until golden brown and ready.

Fried Beef with Potatoes and Mushrooms

Prep time: 20 minutes, cook time: 15 minutes, serves: 3

Ingredients

- 1 pound beef steak
- 1 medium onion, sliced
- 8 oz mushrooms, sliced
- ½ pound potatoes, diced
- Sauce you prefer (Barbecue or Teriyaki)
- Salt and black pepper for seasoning

Directions

1. Wash vegetables, chop onion and mushrooms, dice potatoes.
2. Sprinkle them with salt and pepper.
3. Cut beef steak into 1 inch pieces.
4. In the large mixing bowl combine onion, potatoes, mushrooms and beef. Marinate with sauce and set aside for 15-20 minutes.
5. Preheat the Air Fryer to 350-370°F
6. Put meat and vegetables into the Fryer and cook for 15 minutes.
7. After cooking replace the meal to the serving plate and sprinkle with fresh chopped parsley.

Homemade Cheese Stuffed Burgers

Prep time: 10 minutes, cook time: 20 minutes, serves: 2

Ingredients

- 1 pound finely ground beef
- 2 oz cheddar cheese
- Salt and ground pepper to taste

Directions

1. Take the large mixing bowl and put minced beef. Break it up and season with salt and black pepper.
2. Divide the mince into 4 balls.
3. Cut the cheese into 4 equal pieces.
4. Take half mince from one of the balls and form it into a circle about 2.5 inch wide.
5. Push a piece of the cheese into the center of the mince ball.
6. From the remaining half of mince make the circle with the same width and put on the top. Carefully join the base with cheese and the top and then gently form the burger with your hands.
7. Preheat the Air Fryer to 370°F
8. Cook burgers in the Air Fryer for about 15-20 minutes until they become ready turning halfway through the cooking time.

Beef Meatballs in Red Sauce

Prep time: 15 minutes, cook time: 10 minutes, serves: 3

Ingredients

- 12 oz. (3/4 pounds) ground beef
- 1 small onion
- 1 tablespoon finely chopped fresh parsley
- 1 egg
- ½ tablespoon finely chopped fresh thyme leaves
- 3 tablespoons breadcrumbs
- Pepper and salt to taste
- You can also use 10 oz. tomato sauce

Directions

1. All ingredients put into large bowl and mix. This mixture shapes in 10-12 balls
2. Cook in Air fryer on 390°C for 8 minutes.
3. After that, add tomato sauce and back to the Air fryer on 330°C and cook again for 5 minutes.
4. This meal is actually meatballs, and red sauce is optional. You can serve balls without red sauce if you like.

Meat Rolls with Sage

Prep time: 15 minutes, cook time: 15 minutes, serves: 3-4

Ingredients

- 4 veal cutlets
- 2 cups beef stock
- 1 cup dry white wine
- 8 fresh sage leaves
- 4 slices cured ham
- 1 tablespoon butter
- Freshly ground pepper
- A pinch of salt

Directions

1. Preheat the Air Fryer to 390 F. Pour the beef stock and the wine in a wide pan and bring to a boil over medium heat until it has reduced to one-third of the original amount.
2. Sprinkle salt and pepper on the cutlets and cover them with the sage leaves. Firmly roll the cutlets and wrap a slice of ham around each cutlet.
3. Thinly cover the entire cutlets with butter and place them in the Air Fryer basket. Put the basket in the Fryer and cook for about 10 minutes until nicely brown.
4. Lower the temperature to 320 F and additionally for 5 minutes until almost done. Mix the remainder of the butter with the reduced stock and season the gravy with salt and pepper.
5. Thinly slice the veal rolls and serve them with the gravy. Tastes great with tagliatelle and green beans.

Gentle Thyme Meatloaf

Prep time: 15 minutes, cook time: 25 minutes, serves: 3

Ingredients

- 1 pound ground beef
- 1 egg, beaten
- 3 tablespoons breadcrumbs
- 2 oz salami, chopped
- 1 medium onion, chopped
- 2 tablespoons olive oil
- 1 tablespoon fresh thyme
- Ground pepper and salt to taste

Directions

1. In the large bowl mix ground beef, one egg, breadcrumbs, chopped salami and chopped onion. Add thyme, ground pepper and salt to taste. Stir to combine.
2. Place the beef mixture in the heatproof dish and grease the top with olive oil.
3. Preheat the Air Fryer to 370°F
4. Put the dish with mixture into the Air Fryer cooking basket and set the timer for 25 minutes. Cook until become nicely brown and done.
5. After preparation cut the meatloaf into wedges you like and serve with potatoes or vegetable salad.

Lamb Recipes

Lamb Meatballs Stewed in Yogurt

Prep time: 10 minutes, cook time: 25 minutes, serves: 4

Ingredients for Meatballs

- 1 pound ground lamb
- 1 ½ tablespoon finely chopped parsley,
- 4 ounces ground turkey
- 1 tablespoon finely chopped mint
- 1 teaspoon ground coriander
- 1 teaspoon ground cumin
- 1 teaspoon cayenne pepper
- 2 finely chopped garlic cloves
- ¼ cup olive oil
- 1 teaspoon red chili paste
- 1 egg white
- 1 teaspoon salt

Ingredients for Yogurt

- ½ cup non-fat yogurt – the best is Greek yogurt
- 2 tablespoons buttermilk,
- 1 finely chopped garlic clove
- ¼ cup of mint
- ¼ cup sour cream
- 2 pinches salt

Directions

1. All ingredients for meatballs mix in a large bowl and roll the meatballs between the hands to make balls. It should be the size of golf ball.
2. Cook them in Air fryer at 390°F for 6-8 minutes.
3. Meanwhile, mix ingredients for a yogurt in a bowl and mix them well. Serve it with the meatballs and put a couple of mint leaves and olive oil.

Lamb Chops with Cucumber Raita

Prep time: 1 hour, cook time: 15 minutes, serves: 4

Ingredients

- 4 lamb chops
- 1 teaspoon cumin
- ½ teaspoon chili powder
- 2 tablespoons lime juice
- 4 tablespoons low-fat yogurt
- 1 tablespoon crushed coriander seeds
- 2 teaspoons garam masala
- 1 teaspoon salt Raita

Directions

1. Combine lime juice, yogurt, salt, and spices in the large bowl. Use the mixture to make a coating for the lamb chops. Set aside for about an hour.
2. Meanwhile, preheat the air fryer to 380 F. Place the chops and cook them for approximately 15 minutes.
3. Serve.

Grilled Vegetables with Lamb

Prep time: 10 minutes, cook time: 15 minutes, serves: 2-3

Ingredients

- 4 lamb chops
- ½ bunch fresh mint
- 4 tablespoons olive oil
- 1 small parsnip
- 1 large carrot
- 1 fennel bulb
- Salt and pepper, to taste
- Fresh rosemary

Directions

1. Chop the mint and rosemary. Add 4 tablespoons of olive oil and season the marinade with salt and pepper. Marinate the lamb chops for at least 3 hours.
2. Cut the vegetables into small cubes and leave them to soak in a container of water. Preheat the air fryer to 380 F and sear the lamb chops for 2 minutes. Remove the chops from the basket and cover the bottom with vegetables. Place the lamb chops on top.
3. Cook for another 6 minutes and then serve hot.

Rack of Lamb Crumbed with Herbs

Prep time: 10 minutes, cook time: 25 minutes, serves: 3-4

Ingredients

- 2 pounds rack of lamb
- 2 garlic cloves, minced
- 1 tablespoon paprika
- 2 tablespoon breadcrumbs
- 1 tablespoon freshly chopped rosemary
- 1 tablespoon freshly chopped thyme
- 1 large egg
- 1 tablespoon olive oil
- Salt and black pepper to taste

Directions

1. In the mixing bowl combine minced garlic and olive oil.
2. On the prepared rack of lamb brush the garlic mixture and season with salt, pepper and paprika.
3. In one mixing bowl combine chopped herbs with breadcrumbs and in another one, beat one egg.
4. Now, dip the rack of lamb into the egg and then roll in the herbs mixture.
5. Preheat the air fryer at 250 F.
6. Place the rack of lamb into the air fryer basket and cook for 25 minutes, until the meat becomes ready and crunchy.
7. Serve with mashed potatoes or steamed rice.

Carrot Lamb Meatballs

Prep time: 10 minutes, cook time: 15 minutes, serves 3

Ingredients

- 1 pound ground lamb
- 3 medium carrots, grated
- 3 large eggs, beaten
- 2 garlic cloves, minced
- ½ teaspoon ground pepper
- ½ teaspoon salt

Directions

1. Preheat the air fryer to 380 F
2. Mix all ingredients in the large mixing bowl. Form medium-sized meatballs with hands.
3. Place them in the air fryer and cook for 15 minutes, until ready and crispy.
4. Serve with vegetables or steamed rice.

Roasted Rack of Lamb with a Macadamia Crust

Prep time: 10 minutes, cook time: 30 minutes, serves: 4

Ingredients

- 2 pound rack of lamb
- 1 garlic clove
- 1 tablespoon olive oil
- Salt and pepper, to taste
- ¼ cup unsalted macadamia nuts
- 1 tablespoon breadcrumbs
- 1 tablespoon chopped fresh rosemary
- 1 large egg

Directions

1. Finely chop the garlic and mix it with the olive oil to make garlic oil. Brush the rack of lamb with this oil and season with pepper and salt.
2. Preheat the air fryer to 220 F.
3. Finely chop the nuts and place them into a bowl. Stir in the breadcrumbs and chopped rosemary. Whisk the egg in another bowl.
4. Dip the meat into the egg mixture. Coat the lamb with the macadamia crust. Put the coated lamb rack in the air fryer basket and cook for 25 minutes. When timer beeps, increase the temperature to 390 F and cook for another 5 minutes.
5. Remove the meat and set aside to rest for 10 minutes, covered with aluminum foil.

Spicy Lamb with Pumpkin Wedges

Prep time: 10 minutes, cook time: 30 minutes, serves:3-4

Ingredients

- 1 rack lamb, excess fat trimmed
- 2 tablespoon Dijon mustard
- ½ cup breadcrumbs
- 1 tablespoon dried thyme
- 1 tablespoon dried parsley
- ¼ cup Parmesan cheese, grated
- 1 pound pumpkin, cut into wedges
- Zest from one lemon
- 2 tablespoon olive oil
- Salt and black pepper to taste

Directions

1. Preheat the air fryer to 380 F.
2. Season the rack lamb with salt and pepper from both sides.
3. In the large mixing bowl combine dried herbs, mustard, breadcrumbs, lemon zest, and parmesan cheese. Rub the rack lamb with the mixture.
4. Place the meat into the air fryer and cook for about 20 minutes, turning once during cooking process.
5. Meanwhile, cut the pumpkin into 1-inch wedges. Sprinkle with the olive oil and season with salt. When lamb cooked, transfer meat to a plate and place wedges into the fryer. Cook pumpkin for about 15 minutes, until tender and golden.
6. Serve both rack lamb and pumpkin in the large plate.

Lamb Chops with Garlic Sauce

Prep time 15 minutes, cook time: 22 minutes, serves: 4

Ingredients

- 8 lamb chops
- 4 garlic cloves
- 3 tablespoons olive oil
- 1 tablespoon fresh oregano, chopped
- Salt freshly ground black pepper, to taste

Directions

1. Preheat the air fryer 390 F. Add 1/2 of the olive oil in the air fryer basket and place garlic cloves. Close and cook for 3-5 minutes until golden and fragrant.
2. Meanwhile, mix olive oil with herbs with some salt and pepper. Coat lamb chops with oil mixture and place to the fryer. Cook for about 20 minutes until ready.

Delicious Lamb Patties

Prep time: 8 minutes, cook time: 18 minutes, serves: 4

Ingredients

- 1 pound ground lamb meat
- 2 large eggs, beaten
- ½ teaspoon ground caraway
- ½ teaspoon ground basil
- 1 teaspoon garlic salt

Directions

1. Combine all ingredients in a large mixing bowl. Stir to combine well.
2. Preheat the air fryer to 370 F.
3. Form medium-sized patties from the meat mixture and place them to the air fryer. Cook for about 15-18 minutes, until cooked and browned.
4. Serve and enjoy!

Fish & Seafood Recipes

Fried Shrimps with Celery

Prep time: 15 minutes, cook time: 13 minutes, serves: 3

Ingredients

- 6 to 8 stalks celery
- ½ large carrot, chopped
- 10 to 12 fresh shrimps (quantity depend on your choice)
- 3 clove garlic, finely chopped
- 1 tablespoon olive oil
- 1 tablespoon oyster sauce
- 1 tablespoon soy sauce
- 1 teaspoon sugar
- 1 teaspoon cornstarch
- ¾ to 1 cup water

Directions

1. Put chopped garlic, sliced diagonally celery and sliced carrot into air fryer, pour with oil and cook for 7 minutes.
2. Mix oyster sauce, soy sauce, sugar, cornstarch and water in a bowl. Add this mixture into the air fryer and cook for another 1 minute.
3. Add shrimps and cook for another 5 minutes.

Spring Rolls Stuffed with Shrimps

Prep time: 10 minutes, cook time: 15 minutes, serves: 4

Ingredients

- 4 oz shrimps, cooked
- 12 spring roll wrappers
- 1 teaspoon root ginger, freshly grated
- 2 oz mushrooms, sliced
- 1 egg, beaten
- 1 teaspoon Chinese five-spice powder
- 1 oz bean sprouts
- 1 spring onion
- 1 small carrot, cut into matchsticks
- 1 tablespoon groundnut oil
- 1 tablespoon soy sauce

Directions

1. In the large skillet or wok heat the oil over medium-high heat. Add ginger and mushrooms and cook for 2 minutes. Add the soy sauce, Chinese five-spice powder, bean sprouts, spring onions and carrots. Cook for 1 minute and then set aside to chill. Add the shrimps and toss.
2. Preheat the Air fryer to 370-390 F. Roll up the shrimp mixture in spring roll wrappers, sealing with beaten egg. Brush each roll with oil.
3. Cook in batches in the air fryer basket for 5 minutes.

Delicious Crab Pillows

Prep time: 15 minutes, cook time: 20 minutes, serves: 4

Ingredients

- 2 beaten egg whites
- 1 pound lump crab meat
- 2 tablespoons finely chopped celery
- ¼ finely chopped red bell pepper
- ¼ teaspoon finely chopped tarragon
- ½ teaspoon finely chopped parsley
- ¼ teaspoon finely chopped chives
- 1 tablespoon olive oil
- ¼ cup red onion
- ½ teaspoon cayenne pepper
- ¼ cup sour cream
- ¼ cup mayonnaise

Ingredients for Breading

- 3 beaten eggs
- 1 cup breadcrumbs
- 1 cup flour
- ½ teaspoon salt

Directions

1. Mix onions, celery, peppers and olive oil in a small pan heated on medium-high. Cook for a couple of minutes, until the onion is translucent.
2. Blend breadcrumbs with olive oil and salt to a fine paste.
3. In three bowls prepare eggs, breadcrumbs, and flour. In special bowl mix mayonnaise, crab meat, sour cream, and egg whites.
4. Crab meat mold into balls, roll in flour, eggs and breadcrumbs and put in Air fryer, heated to 390°F, and cook 8-10 minutes.

Fried Crab Chips

Prep time: 7 minutes, cook time: 12 minutes, serves: 3

Ingredients

- 1 pack crab sticks (nearly 1 pound)
- 2 tablespoon extra virgin olive oil
- 2 teaspoon seasoning for you taste - I use curry or Italian seasoning
- 1/3 cup Parmesan cheese, shredded (optional)

Directions

1. First of all, preheat your Air Fryer to 380 F.
2. Cut the crab sticks lengthwise and shred into smaller, but not too small. 1 inch width would be good enough.
3. Sprinkle the Air Fryer basket with the olive oil, place crushed crab sticks and fry for 10-12 minutes until golden. Work in batches if you have many pieces.
4. When ready, replace fried sticks in the plate, season slightly and sprinkle with shredded cheese.

Grilled Stuffed Lobster

Prep time: 10 minutes, cook time: 15 minutes, serves: 3

Ingredients

- 1 lobster
- 2 tablespoons freshly chopped basil
- 1 medium-sized zucchini
- 1 lemon
- 2 tablespoons butter
- Olive oil
- Salt, to taste

Directions

1. Boil the lobster for 5 minutes until nice and red. Place the point of the knife in the groove between the eyes of the lobster. Cut the lobster in half. Then remove the intestinal tract, liver and stomach.
2. Cut the zucchini in long slices and coat them with a little olive oil.
3. Mix chopped basil with butter. Season the mixture with salt, to taste.
4. Preheat the air fryer to 360 F. Add lobster halves, brush with butter and cook for about 6-8 minutes.
5. Remove the lobster from the grill pan and let it rest. Grill the zucchini slices for 4 to 5 minutes at 390 F. Place the lobster and the zucchini slices in a dish and sprinkle with a little lemon juice.

Savory Crab Croquettes

Prep time: 25 minutes, cook time: 20 minutes, serves: 4

Ingredients

- 1 pound lump crab meat
- 1 middle-sized onion, finely chopped
- 1 middle-sized bell pepper, chopped
- 1 stalk celery, chopped
- ¼ teaspoon tarragon, chopped
- ¼ teaspoon chives, chopped
- ½ teaspoon parsley, chopped
- 2 egg whites
- ¼ cup mayonnaise
- ¼ cup sour cream
- ½ cup bread crumbs
- ½ all-purpose flour
- ½ teaspoon black pepper, freshly ground
- A pinch of salt to taste
- ½ teaspoon lime juice, freshly squeezed
- 1 table olive oil

Directions

1. Heat the olive oil in a small pot over medium-high heat, add onions, peppers, and celery. Sauté until translucent for about 4-5 minutes. Remove from heat and chill. Set aside.
2. In a mixing bowl combine all ingredients: crab meat, chopped herbs, mayo, sour cream.
3. In a food processor blend the bread crumbs and salt to a fine crumb.
4. In three separate bowls, set aside eggs, breadcrumbs, and flour.
5. Preheat the Air Fryer to 390°F. Mold crab mixture to the size of golf balls. Place each ball in the flour, then into the eggs, and last the breadcrumbs.
6. Cook half the crab croquettes for 8-10 minutes in the Air Fryer. Work in batches and don't overcrowd. Cook till all crab croquettes are cooked and golden brown.
7. Serve with vegetable salad or dipping sauce.

Thai Fish Cakes with Mango Salsa

Ingredients

- 1 ripe mango
- 1 ½ teaspoons red chili paste
- 1 tablespoon dried coriander
- Juice and zest of 1 lime
- 1 pound white fish fillet (cod, tilapia)
- 1 egg
- 1 green onion, finely chopped
- 2 oz ground coconut
- 1 teaspoon salt

Directions

1. Peel and cut mango into small cubes. Transfer to a bowl and mix with ½ teaspoon red chili paste, coriander and the juice and zest of half a lime.
2. Purée the fish in the food processor and then mix with 1 egg and 1 teaspoon salt and the remainder of the lime zest, red chili paste and the lime juice. Mix with the remainder of the coriander, the green onion and 2 tablespoons coconut.
3. Put the remainder of the coconut on a soup plate. Divide the fish mixture into 12 portions, form them into round cakes and coat them with the coconut.
4. Preheat the air fryer to 360 F and place 6 fish cakes in the basket. Cook for 5-7 minutes until they are golden brown and done.
5. Repeat with remainder of the fish cakes in the same way.
6. Serve the fish cakes with the mango salsa.

Cod Fish Bites

Prep time: 10 minutes, cook time: 8 minutes, serves: 3

Ingredients

- 2 cod fish fillets
- ½ cup all-purpose flour
- 3 eggs
- 2 garlic cloves, minced
- 2 small chili peppers, chopped
- 2 spring onions, chopped
- ¼ teaspoon black pepper
- A pinch of salt

Directions

1. Whisk 3 eggs and add chopped green onion, garlic, and chili. Season with salt and black pepper.
2. Cut the fillets into 2 inch pieces.
3. Coat cod pieces with flour and then dip into the egg mixture.
4. Cook cod pieces into the air fryer for 7-8 minutes at 390 F

Fish Sticks

Ingredients

- 1 pound cod
- 2 large eggs
- 2 cups breadcrumbs
- ½ teaspoon black pepper
- 1 teaspoon salt
- 1 cup all-purpose flour
- 3 tablespoons skimmed milk
- Cheese or Tartar sauce for serving

Directions

1. In a large bowl whisk together milk and eggs. In another bowl place breadcrumbs and in the third bowl put all-purpose flour.
2. Cut cod fish into stripes and season with salt and pepper from both sides. Dip each strip into flour, then into egg mixture, and then into breadcrumbs.
3. Preheat the air fryer to 340 F and cook cod strips for 10-13 minutes, turning once while cooking.
4. Serve with dipping sauce.

Crispy Nachos Shrimps

Prep time: 25 minutes, cook time: 10 minutes, serves: 2

Ingredients

- 20 shrimps
- 2 eggs
- 7 oz nacho flavored chips

Directions

1. Prepare the shrimps. Remove the shells and veins. Apart from the last bit of the tails. Clean and wash them, dry with paper towel.
2. Place eggs in the bowl and whisk.
3. Crush nacho chips in another bowl.
4. Dip each shrimp in the whisked egg and then in the chips crumbs.
5. Preheat the air fryer to 370°F
6. Place the crumbed shrimps to the air fryer basket and cook for 8 minutes, or until they cooked through.
7. Serve with your favorite sauce

Crunchy Fish Taco

Prep time: 10 minutes, cook time: 10 minutes, serves: 4-6

Ingredients

- 12 ounces cod filet
- 1 cup breadcrumbs
- 4-6 flour tortillas
- tablespoons tempura butter
- ½ cup salsa
- ½ cup guacamole
- tablespoons freshly chopped cilantro
- ½ teaspoon salt
- ¼ teaspoon black pepper
- Lemon wedges for garnish

Directions

1. Cut cod filets lengthwise into 2-inch pieces and season with salt and pepper from all sides.
2. Place tempura butter to a bowl and dip each cod piece into it. Then dip filets into breadcrumbs.
3. Preheat the air fryer to 340 F and cook cod sticks for about 10-13 minutes, turning once while cooking.
4. Meanwhile, spread guacamole on each tortilla. Place cod stick to a tortilla and top with chopped cilantro and salsa. Squeeze lemon juice, fold and serve.

Delicate Cod Pillows

Prep time: 10 minutes, cook time: 15 minutes, serves: 4

Ingredients

- 1 pound cod

Ingredients for Breading

- 2 beaten eggs
- 2 tablespoons olive oil
- 1 cup flour
- ¾ cup breadcrumbs
- 1 pinch of salt

Directions

1. First, put Air fryer on 390°F.
2. The cod should be cut on small parts, 1 inch in width and 2.5 inches in length.
3. Blend breadcrumbs with olive oil and put a pinch of salt on it.
4. In three bowls put eggs, a mix of breadcrumbs and oil and flour.
5. Cod roll into breadcrumbs, then eggs and finally in flour. Put in the fryer.
6. Cook 8-10 minutes or until cod has a brown color.

Melt-in-Mouth Salmon Quiche with Broccoli

Prep time: 10 minutes, cook time: 20 minutes, serves: 3-4

Ingredients

- 1/3 pound salmon fillet, cut into 1/2-inch pieces
- 1/2 cup all-purpose flour
- 1/4 cup cold butter
- 3 tablespoon whipping cream
- 2 large eggs
- 1 egg yolk
- 2 teaspoon freshly squeezed lemon juice
- 1 green onion, sliced
- ½ cup broccoli florets
- Salt and ground black pepper to taste

Directions

1. Preheat the air fryer to 380 F.
2. In the mixing bowl combine salmon fillets, salt, ground pepper and lemon juice. Set aside the mixture for 5-10 minutes.
3. In another bowl mix the butter with the egg yolk and flour. Add a tablespoon of cold water and then roll the mixture into a ball.
4. Roll the dough out on a floured surface as needed.
5. Place the batter into the quiche pan and press on edges. Trim the edges.
6. In the large bowl combine the eggs and whipping cream. Add some salt and pepper to taste.
7. Pour the mixture over the dough in the quiche pan and transfer salmon cubes along with the sliced onions and broccoli florets.
8. Place the pan in the air fryer basket and cook for 20 minutes.
9. When ready, top the quiche with extra green onions and serve hot.
10. You can also serve it cold or microwave it if desired.

Miso Tilapia

Ingredients

- 1 pound tilapia fillet
- 2 garlic cloves, minced
- 1 scallion, sliced
- ½ cup miso
- ½ cup mirin
- 1 teaspoon grated ginger

Directions

1. Cut tilapia fillet into 4 equal pieces.
2. Combine miso, mirin, grated ginger, and crushed garlic in the bowl.
3. Soak fish fillets into this mixture and set aside for 20-30 minutes.
4. Cook tilapia in the air fryer for 10-12 minutes at 340 F.
5. Serve with sliced scallions.

Crispy Fish Fillets with Potato Chips

Prep time: 10 minutes, cook time: 14 minutes, serves: 2-3

Ingredients

- 1 pound red potatoes
- ½ pound white fish fillet
- 1 large egg
- 1 tablespoon olive oil
- ½ tablespoon fresh lemon juice
- 1 oz tortilla chips
- Salt and ground black pepper to taste

Directions

1. Preheat the air fryer to 370 F
2. Cut the fish fillets into large pieces and place them to the bowl. Cover fillets lightly with salt, pepper and lemon juice and set aside.
3. Crush the tortilla chips in the plate.
4. In another bowl beat the egg. Dip each piece of fish into the egg and then roll through the tortilla chips. Make sure that fish pieces are covered completely.
5. Clean the potatoes and cut them lengthwise into thin strips. Soak potato chips in the clean water for 15 minutes, and then dry them with kitchen towels. Coat the potato chips with some oil.
6. Place the separator into the air fryer basket and transfer there fish fillets on one side and potatoes on the other.
7. Cook both fish and potatoes for 14 minutes until ready and the skin is crispy and brown.
8. Top with sliced green onions if desired and serve.

Crispy Air Fryer Fish

Prep time: 10 minutes, cook time: 12-15 minutes, serves: 4

Ingredients

- 4 fish fillets (as you desired)
- 1 egg, whisked
- 3 oz breadcrumbs
- 2 tablespoon olive oil
- 1 lemon to serve

Directions

1. In the small bowl whisk one egg and set aside.
2. In another bowl mix oil and breadcrumbs. Stir to combine until becomes loose and crumbly.
3. Preheat the Air Fryer to 360°F
4. Dip prepared fish fillets into whisked egg and then into the breadcrumbs mixture. Make sure that fillets fully breaded.
5. Lay covered fillets in the Air Fryer and cook for 12-15 minutes. Cooking time may vary depending on the fillets thickness.
6. Serve with sliced lemon and enjoy.

Cod with Tomatoes

Prep time: 5 minutes, cook time: 15 minutes, serves: 4

Ingredients

- 4 cod fillets
- 10-12 cherry tomatoes
- 1 tablespoon olive oil
- Salt and pepper to taste
- Basil, parsley or any other fresh herbs of your choice for garnish

Directions

1. Season cod fillets with salt and pepper, sprinkle with olive oil and cook for 12 minutes in the air fryer at 360 F.
2. When almost done, add cherry tomatoes cut on halves. Cook for another 3-4 minutes.
3. Serve cod fillets with grilled tomatoes and herbs of your choice.

Salmon and Cod Lasagna

Prep time: 20 minutes, cook time: 45 minutes, serves 2

Ingredients

- 9 fresh lasagna sheets
- 1 pound salmon
- 1 pound cod
- Juice of 1 lime
- 3.5 oz white wine
- ½ cup cream
- ½ cup milk
- ½ cup grated Cheddar cheese
- 1 small broccoli
- 1 shallot
- 1 tablespoon cornstarch
- 1 tablespoon chopped parsley
- 1 tablespoon chopped chives
- Salt and pepper, to taste

Directions

1. Finely chop the broccoli, shallot, parsley and chives. In a pan, bring the cream, milk, wine and cornstarch to the boil then add the chopped shallot, parsley and chives. As the sauce starts to bind, add the lime juice and season to taste with salt and pepper.
2. Take an ovenproof dish and begin creating the lasagna. Start with some sauce and a first layer of lasagna sheets. Put the sliced broccoli on the first layer and cover with another layer of lasagna sheets. Place the salmon on top, cover with a new layer and put the cod on top. Finish with a layer of sauce and grated cheese.
3. Preheat the air fryer to 320 F and bake the lasagna for 45 minutes. Spoon the lasagna onto a plate and enjoy!

Yummy Shrimps with Bacon

Prep time: 15 minutes, cook time: 15 minutes, serves: 4

Ingredients

- 1 ¼ pounds peeled and deveined tiger shrimp (16 pieces)
- 1 pound thinly sliced pound bacon (also 16 slices) on room temperature

Directions

1. Every shrimp wrap in bacon. To make the job easy and cover the whole shrimp, start from head and finish at the tail. Put shrimps in refrigerator for 20 minutes
2. Cook in Air fryer at 390°F for 5-7 minutes. Then just dry shrimps on paper towel.
3. Serve and enjoy!

Deep Fried Coconut Shrimps

Prep time: 25 minutes, cook time: 20 minutes, serves: 3

Ingredients

- 15-20 large shrimps, deveined and peeled
- 16 oz coconut milk
- 1 cup breadcrumbs
- 1 cup coconut, shredded
- Ground pepper and salt for seasoning

Directions

1. Add a pinch of salt in a coconut milk, whisk and set aside.
2. Combine breadcrumbs with shredded coconut, add salt and pepper to taste.
3. Preheat the Air Fryer to 330°F
4. Dip each shrimp in the milk mixture, then coat with coconut mix.
5. Put shrimps in the fryer and cook for nearly 20 minutes.
6. Serve and enjoy!

Cod Fish Teriyaki with Oyster Mushrooms

Prep time: 5 minutes, cook time: 12 minutes, serves: 2-3

Ingredients

- 1 pound cod fish cut into 1-inch thickness pieces
- 6 pieces Oyster mushrooms, sliced
- 1 Wong Bok leaf, sliced
- 2 garlic cloves, coarsely chopped
- 1 tablespoon olive oil
- A pinch of salt
- Steamed rice for serving

Ingredients for Teriyaki sauce

- 2 tablespoon mirin
- 2 tablespoon soy sauce
- 2 tablespoon sugar

Directions

1. Take a large baking pan suitable for your air fryer and grease it with the little oil.
2. Toss your mushroom, garlic and salt with 1 tablespoon of oil in a baking pan. Lay the cod fish slices on top of mushrooms.
3. Preheat the Air Fryer at 360 F and place the baking pan into the air fryer. Cook for 5 minutes. Then, stir the mushrooms to prevent sticking and burning. Some mushroom parts may have browned slightly and it is ok.
4. Drizzle Teriyaki sauce over cod fish slices. Fry for another 5 minutes.
5. When ready, transfer cod fish slices to serving plate.
6. Stir the mushrooms with the remaining sauce in the baking pan.
7. Serve with steamed rice.

Tender Tuna Nuggets

Prep time: 130 minutes, cook time: 10 minutes, serves: 3

Ingredients

- 2 cans tuna (10-12 oz)
- ½ cup breadcrumbs
- 3 tablespoon olive oil
- 2 tablespoon parsley, chopped
- 1 egg
- 2 teaspoon Dijon mustard
- Ground pepper and salt to taste

Directions

1. Mix tuna, olive oil, parsley, egg and mustard in a large bowl.
2. Form tuna mixture into nuggets and place them on the baking sheet.
3. Cool nuggets in the fridge for 2 hours
4. Preheat the Air Fryer to 350°F.
5. Put frozen nuggets to the Fryer and cook for 10 minutes.

Delicate Halibut Steak with Garlic

Prep time: 10 minutes, cook time: 30 minutes, serves: 3

Ingredients

- 1 pound halibut steak
- Marinade
- 2/3 cup soy sauce
- ¼ cup sugar
- ½ cup Japanese cooking wine – miring
- 2 tablespoons lime juice
- 1 smashed garlic clove
- ¼ cup orange juice
- ¼ teaspoon ginger ground
- ¼ teaspoon crushed red pepper flakes

Directions

1. All ingredients mix in a saucepan and make a fine marinade
2. Boil it and then reduce by half, cool both halves
3. Once half put with the halibut in releasable bag and put in refrigerator for 30 minutes
4. Put in Air fryer on 390°F and cook for 10-12 minutes
5. The other half of the marinade put on the cooked steak and serve with white rice.

Salmon in Delicious Sauce

Prep time: 15 minutes, cook time: 15 minutes, serves: 4

Ingredients

- 1 ½ pounds salmon (each should be 6 oz. and prepare 4 pieces)
- 2 teaspoons olive oil
- Salt to taste

Ingredients for Sauce

- ½ cup non-fat yogurt – Greek yogurt is the best for this meal
- ½ cup sour cream
- 2 tablespoons finely chopped dill
- Salt to taste

Directions

1. Salmon cut into small pieces – it should be 6 ounces portions. Put teaspoon oil on top of it and salt.
2. Cook the salmon in Air fryer at 270°F for 20-23 minutes
3. Mix sour cream, yogurt, chopped dill and salt in large bowl and pour cooked salmon with this sauce. Serve with chopped dill and salt.

Salmon with Pesto and Roasted Tomatoes

Prep time: 5 minutes, cook time 10 minutes, serves: 4

Ingredients

- 4 salmon steaks
- 4 tablespoons pesto
- 1 pound pasta
- 8 large prawns
- 9 oz cherry tomatoes
- 1 medium lemon
- Olive oil
- Fresh thyme

Directions

1. Boil the water for the pasta and add some salt. Add the pasta when the water boils.
2. Meanwhile, take an ovenproof dish and coat with one tablespoon of pesto.
3. Place sliced salmon in the dish and spread on the rest of the pesto.
4. Pour on two tablespoons of olive oil. Halve the tomatoes and put them with the salmon.
5. Place the prawns on the salmon, drizzle with lemon juice and grill air fry at 390 F for 8 minutes. Drain the pasta and serve with the salmon and prawns.
6. Enjoy.

Sweet and Tender Salmon Sugar Glazed

Prep time: 7 minutes, cook time: 15 minutes, serves: 3

Ingredients

- 3 salmon filets
- 1 tablespoon brown sugar
- 2 tablespoons coconut oil, melted
- Salt and pepper to taste

Directions

1. Combine in a middle bowl coconut oil with brown sugar, mix and season with salt and pepper.
2. Preheat the Air Fryer to 340-360°F
3. Dip salmon filets to the mixture. Be careful and try not to destroy tender salmon.
4. Put the glazed salmon into the air fryer and cook for approximately 15 minutes until ready.
5. Serve with vegetables you like or salad.

Salmon Steaks with Soy Sauce

Prep time 5 minutes, cook time: 10 minutes, serves: 3

Ingredients

- 1 pound salmon steaks
- ¼ cup brown sugar
- 4 tablespoon soy sauce
- 2 tablespoons olive oil
- 2 tablespoons fresh lemon juice
- 3 tablespoons dry white wine
- Lemon wedges for serving
- Salt to taste

Directions

1. In a medium bowl combine soy sauce, olive oil, brown sugar, wine and lemon juice. Stir until the sugar dissolves.
2. Dip salmon steaks into the mixture, leave for 10 minutes.
3. Preheat the Air Fryer to 380°F
4. Then place salmon into a heatproof dish, season with salt to taste, put into the Fryer cooking basket and prepare for 10 minutes.
5. Serve with lemon wedges and enjoy.

Savory Salmon Fishcakes

Prep time: 5 minutes, cook time: 8 minutes, serves: 4

Ingredients

- 1 pound cooked salmon
- 2 pounds cold mashed potatoes
- ¼ cup capers
- 3 tablespoon dill, chopped
- 2 tablespoon olive oil
- Salt and ground pepper to taste

Directions

1. In the large mixing bowl combine the salmon and mashed potato. Stir well. Add dill, capers, season with salt and pepper to taste.
2. Form the fishcakes with hands from the mixture and lay to a baking sheet. Brush each patty with olive oil.
3. Preheat the air fryer to 360 F.
4. Place the fishcakes into the air fryer basket and cook for about 6-8 minutes, until tender inside and crispy outside.
5. Serve and enjoy!

Asian Salmon with Fried Rice

Prep time: 5 minutes, cook time: 10 minutes, serves: 3-4

Ingredients

- 1 pound salmon fillet
- 2 cup cooked rice
- 3 large eggs, beaten
- 2 tablespoon olive oil
- 3 garlic cloves, minced
- 2 tablespoon frozen mixed vegetables
- 2 sprig spring onions, chopped
- 1 ½ teaspoons sambal chili
- 1 tablespoon light soy sauce
- 3 teaspoon seasoning for salmon (as you prefer)
- A pinch of salt

Directions

1. Season fish fillets on both sides and set aside. Cook salmon fillet skin side up at 360 F for couple minutes till 80% done. Replace to a large plate.
2. Add some oil to the air fryer basket and fry garlic till fragrant, 1-2 minutes. Add the frozen mixed vegetables and cook for a minute more. Add salmon pieces.
3. Then add all the rice and stir fry quickly to combine. Pour in the soy sauce and sambal chili. Mix well. Make some space in the middle of the rice and crack the eggs. Allow to set for 30 seconds then combine with all the rice. Keep tossing to keep things going. Add the chopped spring onions.
4. Continue frying on high heat until salmon ready and rice golden.

Oil-free Fried Fishcakes

Prep time: 35 minutes, cook time: 15 minutes, serves: 4

Ingredients

- 1 pound any white fish, boneless and cooked
- 1 cup mashed potatoes
- 3 tablespoon skimmed milk
- 3 tablespoon unsalted butter
- 2 table spoon all-purpose flour
- 1 tablespoon freshly chopped dill
- 1 tablespoon freshly chopped parsley
- A pinch of salt
- ¼ teaspoon black pepper, freshly ground

Directions

1. Combine mashed potatoes, cooked fish, and chopped herbs. Season with salt and pepper and stir to combine.
2. Add the butter and then milk until you have a nice consistency. Add a little flour and then make patty cakes with hands.
3. Refrigerate fishcakes for an hour to make them solid.
4. Cook fish bites for 12-15 minutes at 390 F, until golden.
5. Serve with cooked rice or vegetables!

Dessert Recipes

Apple Wedges with Cinnamon

Prep time: 10 minutes, cook time: 15 minutes, serves: 4

Ingredients

- 4 golden apples (or as you like)
- 2 tablespoons sunflower oil
- 1/2 cup ready-to-eat dried apricots, finely chopped
- 1-2 tablespoons superfine sugar
- ½ teaspoon ground cinnamon, or to taste

Directions

1. Wash apples, dry with paper towels, peel them. Cut each one into quarters and remove and discard the cores. Cut each apple quarter in half to make 2 even wedges (each whole apple is cut into 8 even wedges).
2. Place the apple wedges in a large bowl, add the oil and toss to mix until the apples are coated all over.
3. Put the apple wedges in the air fryer and cook for 12-15 minutes.
4. Add the apricots and cook for another 3 minutes, or until the apples are tender.
5. In another bowl mix together the sugar and cinnamon.
6. Serve the hot cooked apple wedges with a sprinkling of cinnamon sugar.

Tip: You can serve apple widgets with vanilla ice cream or Greek yogurt.

Flourless Lemon Cupcakes

Prep time: 10 minutes, cook time: 20 minutes, serves: 5-6

Ingredients

- 1 cup Greek yoghurt
- 8 oz soft cheese
- 2 large eggs, beaten
- 1 egg yolk
- 1 teaspoon vanilla extract
- 1 large lemon (juice and zest)
- ¼ cup caster sugar

Directions

1. In the large bowl mix together the Greek yoghurt and the soft cheese until they are nice and creamy and are like a mayonnaise. Use the wooden spoon or hand mixer. Beat the eggs and mix again. Add the sugar, vanilla extract and the lemon and mix again.
2. You need to get a creamy mixture and you need to fill 6 cupcake cases with the contents. Put the rest to one side for later.
3. Preheat your Air Fryer to 360 F and cook the cupcakes for 10 minutes. Then increase the temperature up to 390 F and cook for a further 10 minutes.
4. Meanwhile, the cupcakes are cooking remove the contents of your bowl into a cupcake nozzle and place in the fridge for 10 minutes.
5. When the cupcakes are done allow them to chill for 10 minutes.
6. When they are cool using the nozzle create the top layer of your cupcakes. Refrigerate for 2-4 hours so that your cupcake topping has time to properly set and then decorate with spare lemon.

Fried Apple Dumplings

Prep time: 10 minutes, cook time: 25 minutes, serves: 3

Ingredients

- 2-3 medium apples
- 2 tablespoon raisins
- 1 ½ tablespoon brown sugar
- 2 sheets puff pastry
- 3 tablespoon butter, melted
- 1 teaspoon icing sugar for topping

Directions

1. Core and peel apples.
2. Mix the raisins and the brown sugar.
3. Put each apple on one of the puff pastry sheet then fill the core with the raisin and sugar mixture. Fold the pastry around the apple so it is fully covered.
4. Place the apple dumplings on a small sheet of foil (to avoid any juices escape from the apple and don't fall into the air fryer). Brush the dough with the melted butter.
5. Cook apples for about 20-25 minutes at 370 F, until becomes golden brown and the apples are soft.
6. Top with icing sugar and serve hot.

Crispy Peach Slices

Prep time: 5 minutes, cook time: 30 minutes, serves: 4

Ingredients

- 2 large peaches, sliced
- 2-3 tablespoons sugar
- 2 tablespoons all-purpose flour
- 2 tablespoons oats
- 2 tablespoons unsalted butter
- ¼ teaspoon vanilla extract
- 1 teaspoon cinnamon

Directions

1. In a large mixing bowl mix peach slices, sugar, vanilla extract, and cinnamon. Transfer to a baking pan.
2. Place baking pan to an air fryer and cook for20 minutes on 290 F.
3. Meanwhile, in another bowl mix oats, flour, and unsalted butter. Stir to combine.
4. When peach slices cooked, open the lid and top peaches with butter mixture. Close the fryer and cook for 10 minutes more on 300-310 F.
5. When ready, set aside for 5-10 minutes to become crispy.
6. Serve with ice-cream.

Tasty Apple Chips

Prep time: 15 minutes, cook time: 20 minutes, serves: 4

Ingredients

- 4 granny smith apples
- 1 cup rolled oats (quick cook if possible)
- 1 teaspoon butter, melted
- 1 teaspoon cinnamon
- 2 teaspoon brown sugar
- 1 teaspoon olive oil

Directions

1. Wash and dry apples, peel them and remove cores.
2. Mix melted butter, brown sugar and oats.
3. Cut apples into slices, put into the air fryer, sprinkle mixture around the apples and cook for 10-15 minutes.

Indian Banana Chips

Prep time: 10 minutes, cook time: 15 minutes, serves: 3

Ingredients

- 4 raw bananas
- ½ teaspoon turmeric powder
- ½ teaspoon Chat Masala
- 1 teaspoon salt
- ½ cup water
- 1 teaspoon olive oil

Directions

1. Preheat your Air Fryer to 350 F
2. Combine turmeric powder and salt with water smoothly.
3. Cover out the skin of banana and slice them. Smear it with the turmeric mixture. Leave bananas in this mixture for 5-10 minutes and then drain and finally, make the chips dry.
4. Brush a little bit oil on the chips. Put them into the air fryer and cook the chips for 15 minutes.
5. Finally, mix salt and Chat Masala with this fried banana and serve immediately.

Mixed Berry Pleasure

Prep time: 10 minutes, cook time: 18 minutes, serves: 4

Ingredients

- 4 granny smith apples
- ½ pound fresh strawberries
- 1 mango
- 1 cup fresh cranberries
- 2 teaspoon honey
- 1 teaspoon cinnamon
- 1 teaspoon nutmeg
- 1 teaspoon coconut oil

Directions

1. Peel and core apples, slice them.
2. Cut strawberries in half.
3. Dice the mango.
4. Combine sliced apples, strawberries, mango and cranberries in a bowl with oil.
5. Put everything in the air fryer and cook for 7-10 minutes.
6. Mix honey, cinnamon and nutmeg, add to the air fryer and cook for other 7-8 minutes.

Pineapple Cake

Prep time: 10 minutes, cook time: 35 minutes, serves: 4

Ingredients

- 2 cups self raising flour
- ¼ pound butter
- tablespoons sugar
- ½ pound pineapple, chopped
- ½ cup pineapple juice
- oz dark chocolate, grated
- 1 large egg
- 2 tablespoons skimmed milk

Directions

1. Preheat the air fryer to 370 F and grease a cake tin.
2. In the mixing bowl combine butter and flour. Mix well until the mixture will be like breadcrumbs. Add sugar, diced pineapple, juice, and crushed dark chocolate. Mix well.
3. In another bowl mix egg and milk. Pour to the flour mixture and prepare a soft pastry.
4. Transfer the mixture to a greased tin and place to an air fryer. Cook for about 35-40 minutes, then serve and enjoy.

Pumpkin Cake

Prep time: 15 minutes, cook time: 30 minutes, serves: 3

Ingredients

- 1 egg
- 6 tablespoons milk
- 7 oz flour
- 3 oz brown sugar
- 5 oz pumpkin puree
- Pinch of salt
- Cooking spray

Directions

1. Mix pumpkin puree and brown sugar in a bowl.
2. Add one egg and whisk until smooth.
3. Mix the flour and salt. Pour milk and combine again.
4. Take the baking tin and coat with cooking spray.
5. Pour the batter into the baking tin.
6. Preheat the Air Fryer to 350°F
7. Put the baking tin to the air fryer basket and set the timer for 15 minutes.
8. Enjoy.

Tip: you can add a pinch of cinnamon to add flavor and interesting taste.

Roasted Pumpkin Seeds with Cinnamon

Prep time: 15 minutes, cook time: 20 minutes, serves: 2

Ingredients

- 1 cup pumpkin raw seeds
- 1 tablespoon ground cinnamon
- 2 tablespoons brown sugar
- 1 cup water
- 1 tablespoon olive oil

Directions

1. Add pumpkin seeds, cinnamon and water in a sauté pot. Stir to combine and heat the mixture over high heat. Boil for 2-3 minutes. Drain water and transfer seeds to a kitchen towel. Dry for 20-30 minutes.
2. In the mixing bowl combine sugar, dried seeds, a pinch of cinnamon and 1 tablespoon of olive oil. Mix well.
3. Preheat the air fryer to 340 F and transfer seed mixture to the fryer basket. Cook for 15 minutes, shaking couple times.
4. Enjoy.

Blackberry & Apricot Crumble Cake

Prep time: 10 minutes, cook time: 20 minutes, serves: 4-5

Ingredients

- ½ pound fresh or dried apricots
- ¼ fresh or frozen blackberries
- ½ cup plain flour
- 1 tablespoon lemon juice
- 3 tablespoon sugar
- 2 tablespoon butter
- A pinch of salt

Directions

1. Discard the stones from the apricots (if you use fresh apricots). Cut the apricots into cubes and place in the mixing bowl. Sprinkle with lemon juice and 1 tablespoon of sugar. Set aside.
2. In another bowl combine flour, a pinch of salt, the remainder of the sugar and butter. Pour in one tablespoon cold water and mix well. You should receive crumbly mixture.
3. Preheat the air fryer to 380 F.
4. Grease the cake tin with olive oil and lay the fruit mixture in the tin.
5. Distribute the crumbly pastry over the fruit and press the top layer.
6. Put the cake tip into the air fryer basket and cook for 20 minutes, until golden and well done.
7. Serve with any topping you prefer: honey, whipped cream or chocolate sauce.

Delicious Fried Bananas

Prep time: 3 minutes, cook time: 8 minutes, serves: 2

Ingredients

- 2 large bananas
- ½ cup plain flour
- 2 eggs, whisked
- ¾ cup breadcrumbs
- ½ cup cinnamon sugar
- 1 tablespoon olive oil
- A pinch of salt

Directions

1. Take 4 bowls and place separately: flour with salt, whisked eggs, breadcrumbs, and cinnamon sugar.
2. Peel bananas and cut them into thirds. Evenly cover bananas with the flour, then with eggs, and finally with breadcrumbs.
3. Preheat the Air Fryer to 360°F
4. Sprinkle covered bananas with olive oil and put into the Air Fryer. Cook for 4-5 minutes, and then make a shake to move bananas. Cook for another 4-5 minutes.
5. Remove the bananas and through then directly into the cinnamon sugar.
6. Get them cool for a minute and eat!

British Lemon Tarts

Ingredients

- ½ cup butter
- ½ pound plain flour
- 3 tablespoons sugar
- 1 large lemon (juice and zest taken)
- 2 tablespoons lemon curd
- A pinch of nutmeg

Directions

1. In a large mixing bowl combine butter, flour and sugar. Mix well until the mixture will be like breadcrumbs. Then add lemon zest and juice, a pinch of nutmeg and mix again. If needed, add couple tablespoons of water to make really soft dough.
2. Take little pastry tins and sprinkle with flour. Add dough and top with sugar or lemon zest.
3. Preheat the air fryer to 360 F and cook mini lemon tarts for 15 minutes, until ready.
4. Serve and enjoy.

Amazing Coconut Cookies

Ingredients

- 1 egg
- 3 tablespoons dried coconut
- 3 oz butter
- 2 oz brown sugar
- 1 teaspoon vanilla extract
- 2 oz white chocolate
- 5 oz flour

Directions

1. In the medium bowl mix butter and brown sugar. Cream until fluffy.
2. Add one egg, vanilla extract and stir to combine.
3. Crush the chocolate into small pieces. Add them to the mixture.
4. Roll small balls with hands.
5. Roll these balls in the dried coconut cover.
6. Place balls on the baking sheet.
7. Preheat the Air Fryer to 370°F
8. Bake coconut balls for 8 minutes.
9. Lower the temperature to 280-300°F and cook for another 4 minutes.
10. Serve and enjoy!

Chocolate Chips Cookies

Prep time: 5 minutes, cook time: 8-9 minutes, serves: 5-6

Ingredients

- 5 tablespoon unsalted butter
- 4 tablespoon brown sugar
- 1 cup self raising flour or less
- 4 oz chocolate
- 1-2 tablespoon honey
- 1 tablespoon skimmed milk
- A pinch of vanilla extract

Directions

1. Combine softened butter, sugar and mix together until they are light and fluffy. Stir in honey, flour and vanilla extract and mix well.
2. Using a rolling pin smash up your chocolate so that they are a mix of medium and really small chocolate chunks. Add the chocolate to the mixture. Also pour in the milk and stir well.
3. Preheat the Air Fryer to 370 F. Spoon the cookies into the air fryer on a baking sheet and cook for 5-6 minutes. Reduce the temperature to 330 F and cook additionally for 2 minutes so that they can cook in the middle.

Classic Brownies

Prep time: 20 minutes, cook time: 30 minutes, serves: 6

Ingredients

- ½ cup butter
- 3.5 oz dark chocolate
- 3.5 oz white chocolate
- 3 large eggs
- ½ cup sugar
- 1 tablespoon vanilla extract
- 3.5 oz flour
- 5 oz pecan nuts, chopped
- Salt, to taste

Directions

1. Preheat the air fryer to 350 F. Melt half of the butter with the dark chocolate in a thick-bottomed pan, and melt the white chocolate in another pan with the rest of the butter. Leave to chill.
2. Using the mixer, mix eggs briefly with the sugar and vanilla. Divide the flour into 2 portions and add a pinch of salt to each. Beat half of the egg-sugar mixture through the dark chocolate. Then add in half of the flour and half of the nuts and mix.
3. Do the same with the white chocolate mixture. Pour the white and brown brownie mixture into two different sides of the cake tin. Use a spatula to partially mix the two colors, creating a swirl.
4. Bake the brownies for about 30 minutes. When ready, the surface should be dry to touch.

Roast Pineapple and Figs in Australian Honey

Prep time: 10 minutes, cook time: 15 minutes, serves: 4

Ingredients

- 1 medium pineapple
- 4 fresh figs
- 1 tablespoon lemon juice
- 3 tablespoon honey
- 1 pinch powdered cinnamon

Directions

1. Cut off the upper and lower parts of the pineapple. Cut it into eight stripes. Peel and core and chop pineapple into cubes.
2. Put pineapple cubes into the air fryer, pour in two tablespoons of honey and cook for 10 minutes.
3. Wash and dry figs, cut them into quarters.
4. Add the figs remaining tablespoon of honey, fresh lemon juice and cinnamon. Cook for 3-5 minutes.
5. Serve the pineapple and figs with vanilla ice cream.

Cherry Clafoutis

Prep time: 15 minutes, cook time: 25 minutes, serves: 4

Ingredients

- ½ cup fresh or frozen cherries
- 2 tablespoons vodka
- 3 tablespoons flour
- 2 tablespoons sugar
- 1 large egg
- 4 oz sour cream

Directions

1. Pit the cherries and mix them in a bowl with vodka.
2. Preheat the air fryer to 350 F. In another bowl mix the flour with the sugar, a pinch of salt, the egg and the sour cream until the dough is smooth and thick.
3. Spoon the batter into the buttered cake pan. Place the cherries evenly over the top of the batter and place the remaining butter in small chunks evenly on top. Put the cake pan into the air fryer and cook for 25 minutes. Cook until golden brown and done.

Fried Bananas with Ice Cream

Prep time: 5 minutes, cook time: 15 minutes, serves: 2

Ingredients

- 2 bananas
- 1 tablespoon butter
- 1 scoop brown sugar
- 2 scoops bread crumbs
- 2 scoops vanilla ice cream

Directions

1. Melt butter in air fryer in one minute.
2. Mix sugar and bread crumbs in a bowl.
3. Cut bananas into 1-inch slices and add to sugar mixture. Mix well.
4. Put covered bananas into air fryer and cook for 10-15 minutes.
5. Serve warm and add ice cream.

Eggless Air Fryer Wheat Cookies

Prep time: 15 minutes, cook time: 15 minutes, serves: 3-4

Ingredients

- 1 cup whole wheat flour
- ½ cup castor sugar
- ½ cup unsalted butter
- ½ cup skimmed milk
- ¼ teaspoon baking powder
- 2 teaspoon chocolate chips

Directions

1. In the large mixing bowl combine wheat flour, baking powder and unsalted butter. Then, add chocolate chips, castor sugar, pour in milk and knead the dough until it becomes soft and smooth.
2. Place the dough into the refrigerator for 10-15 minutes. After that, roll up some small balls, approximately 1 inch in diameter. Flatten the balls to make cookies.
3. Preheat the air fryer to 360 F. Place cookies into the air fryer basket and cook for about 10 minutes.
4. When ready, remove cookies from the fryer and give them chill for about 10-15 minutes.
5. Serve cookies and enjoy!

Classic Soufflé with Vanilla

Prep time: 40 minutes, cook time: 20 minutes, serves: 5

Ingredients

- ¼ cup flour
- 1 cup milk
- ¼ cup softened butter
- 2 teaspoons vanilla extract
- ¼ cup sugar
- 5 egg whites
- 1 vanilla bean
- 1 ounce sugar
- 4 egg yolks
- 1 teaspoon cream of tartar

Directions

1. First, flour and butter should be mixed in a smooth paste. Heat the milk aside and dissolve the sugar. Before the boiling add vanilla bean. If you are not sure that it will be smooth you can use kitchen wire whisk and beat it to avoid lumps. It needs about seven minutes for cooking.
2. While is still warm put vanilla bean and put in an ice bath for 10 minutes to cool it.
3. Now is time for butter. Coat it with a pinch of sugar. The egg yolks quickly beat in another bowl with vanilla extract and all add in cooled milk.
4. Beat egg whites, sugar, and cream of tartar separately and add egg white in cream when it's smooth.
5. Cook in the fryer on 330°F for 14-16 minutes. After is finished, you can serve this with chocolate powder and sauce on the top.
6. This recipe is for 4 small cups, so you should separate it into four portions and cook them separately in air fryer.

Sweety Blueberry Muffins

Prep time: 25 minutes, cook time: 15 minutes, serves: 4

Ingredients

- 3 oz flour
- 1 egg
- 3 oz milk
- 2 oz butter, melted
- 4 oz dried blueberries
- 1 teaspoon cinnamon
- 3 tablespoons brown sugar

Directions

1. In the large bowl sift the flour, add cinnamon, sugar and stir to combine.
2. In another bowl whisk one egg with milk and add melted butter. Mix well and stir this mixture in the flour.
3. Add dried blueberries to the mixture.
4. Put the batter into the muffin cups.
5. Preheat the Air Fryer to 380°F
6. Carefully place filled muffin cups to the air fryer basket and set the timer to 15 minutes.
7. Bake muffins until they become golden brown.
8. Cool and serve.

Awesome Chocolate Cake

Prep time: 10 minutes, cook time: 15 minutes, serves: 4-5

Ingredients

- ¼ cup butter
- 3 tablespoon caster sugar
- 3 tablespoon all-purpose flour
- 1 large egg
- 1 tablespoon apricot or apple jam
- 1 tablespoon cocoa powder
- Some icing sugar for garnish
- Dash of salt

Directions

1. First, you need to preheat the air fryer to 360 F.
2. In the large mixing bowl, whisk caster sugar and butter. You need to receive light creamy mixture. Add the jam and beat the egg into the bowl, then add cocoa powder, all-purpose flour and salt. Stir to combine evenly.
3. Spray some non-stick spray onto the ring cake tin.
4. Pour the mixture into the ring tin and level it with the spoon.
5. Place the tin in the preheated air fryer basket and cook for about 15 minutes.
6. When ready, check the cake with the help of the toothpick - put it in the cake and pull it out clean.
7. Let the cake rest for 10 minutes, and then sprinkle the top of the cake with icing sugar and serve.

Little Apple Pie

Prep time: 5 minutes, cook time: 17 minutes, serves: 8

Ingredients

- 2 large apples
- ½ cup plain flour
- 2 tablespoons unsalted butter
- 1 tablespoon sugar
- ½ teaspoon cinnamon

Directions

1. Preheat the air fryer to 360 F
2. In the large mixing bowl combine flour and butter. Stir to combine. Add sugar and mix well. Add couple tablespoons of water and prepare nice dough. Mix until you get a smooth texture.
3. Take small pastry tins and cover with butter. Fill tins with pastry.
4. Peel and core apples. Dice them. Place diced apples over the pastry and sprinkle with sugar and cinnamon.
5. Transfer pastry tins to an air fryer and cook for 15-17 minutes, until ready.
6. Serve with whipped cream or ice cream.

Delicious Banana Cake with Honey

Prep time: 15 minutes, cook time: 30 minutes, serves: 3-4

Ingredients

- 2 tablespoon honey
- ¼ cup butter
- 1 large banana, mashed
- 1 cup plain flour
- 1 large egg, beaten
- A pinch of cinnamon
- 4 tablespoon brown sugar
- Dash of salt to taste
- Honey for serving

Directions

1. Preheat the air fryer to 370 F.
2. Prepare the ring cake tin - cover it with some non-stick spray.
3. In the mixing bowl combine the sugar with butter. Then, add the honey, beaten egg, mashed banana. Mix well and then add cinnamon, plain flour and salt. Combine evenly; you need to receive smooth mixture for the batter.
4. Transfer the mixture into the tin and place it to the air fryer basket.
5. Set the timer to 30 minutes. When ready, check the cake condition with the toothpick.
6. Give it 5 minutes to rest and then serve with honey.

Banana Bread

Ingredients

- ½ ripe banana, peeled
- 2 eggs
- 4 tablespoon unsalted butter, plus 2 teaspoons
- ¾ cup flour, plus some more for dusting the loaf pan
- 1/3 cup pecans, lightly toasted and chopped
- ¼ cup brown sugar
- ¼ cup granulated sugar
- ¾ teaspoon vanilla extract
- 1 teaspoon ground cinnamon
- ¼ teaspoon ground nutmeg
- A pinch of salt
- ¼ teaspoon baking soda
- 1/8 teaspoon baking powder

Directions

1. Grease the loaf pan with 2 teaspoons of butter and dust the inner side with flour. Set aside.
2. In a mixing bowl place a half of the banana and brown sugar. Combine using the back of the spoon.
3. Add eggs, granulated sugar, vanilla extract, cinnamon, nutmeg, and salt and whisk thoroughly to combine.
4. Sift in flour, baking soda and baking powder. Stir to combine.
5. Pour the batter into the prepared loaf pan and sprinkle with pecans.
6. Preheat the Air Fryer to 310-330°F
7. Place the loaf pan into the Fryer and cook for 30 minutes.
8. Then check the bread with a cake tester or wooden skewer and cook more until tester will come out clean.
9. Remove from the loaf pan, cut into slices and serve with honey or another topping.

Conclusion

Thank you again for downloading my cookbook! I Hope this book helps you to know more interesting and tasty recipes or inspire you to create your own unique dishes.

Note from the author:

If you've enjoyed this book, I'd greatly appreciate if you could leave an honest review on Amazon.
Reviews are very important to us authors, and it only takes a minute for to post.

Thank you!

Made in the USA
Lexington, KY
06 January 2018